HOW TO PREPARE A RESULTS-DRIVEN BUSINESS PLAN

HOW TO PREPARE A RESULTS-DRIVEN BUSINESS PLAN

GREGORY J. MASSARELLA
PATRICK D. ZORSCH
DANIEL D. JACOBSON
MARC J. RITENHOUSE

GRANT THORTON

*Accountants and
Management Consultants*

amacom
American Management Association
New York • Atlanta • Boston • Chicago • Kansas City • San Francisco • Washington, D.C.
Brussels • Toronto • Mexico City

This book is available at a special
discount when ordered in bulk quantities.
For information, contact Special Sales Department,
AMACOM, a division of American Management Association,
135 West 50th Street, New York, NY 10020.

This publication is designed to provide accurate and authorita-
tive information in regard to the subject matter covered. It is sold
with the understanding that the publisher is not engaged in ren-
dering legal, accounting, or other professional service. If legal ad-
vice or other expert assistance is requried, the services of a
competent professional person should be sought.

Library of Congress Cataloging-in-Publication Data

How to prepare a results-driven business plan / Greg J. Massarella . . . [et al.].
    p.   cm.
    Includes index.
    ISBN 0-8144-5136-5
    1. Corporate planning.
    HD30.28.H694   1993
    658.4'012—dc20   93-9711
                                        CIP

Printing number

10 9 8 7 6 5 4 3 2 1

Contents

PART ONE

Chapter 1
Business Planning: Introduction and Objectives

Since the late 1980s, the economic downturn and the banking crisis have combined to profoundly change the business climate in the United States. The acquisition of funds via bank loan or investor capital has become significantly more complex, formalized, and competitive than ever before. Deals that are consummated solely on the basis of a company's track record, its industry, or the banker/investor's relationship with its principals are a thing of the past. In most lending/investing situations, companies are now subjected to intense scrutiny, and this almost always involves a detailed analysis by the lender or investor of a company's written business plan.

Organizations that engage in continual business planning, whether for internal or external use, have always enjoyed the competitive advantage that a well-charted strategic direction provides. Now, however, the ability to draw up, present, and defend a well-written and documented business plan that supports strategy may well determine whether a company is able to acquire the funding necessary to start up, continue, or grow its operations.

Numerous books espousing the latest theory in strategic business thinking are published each year. There are also a number of books that deal specifically with creating business plans; however, most emphasize the theory underlying each decision implicit in any plan. This book, by contrast, is directed away from theory and toward the continuing broad-based need for a true how-to book—a pragmatic, process-oriented text that will serve as a reference resource for the business owner, chief executive officer, chief financial officer, or divisional general manager who must actually prepare a plan for the bank, an investor, internal use, or any of the several other purposes discussed in more detail in Chapter 2.

Targeted Planning

The business plan most appropriate for use by a banker in determining whether to lend a company money for working capital is not necessarily the type plan to give to a potential investor. This book was written to help business planners identify who their potential readers are, how the plan will be used, and, most important, how to shift the plan's emphasis so that it will match up with the reader/user's hot buttons. This discussion begins in Chapter 2 and is expanded on as appropriate throughout the book.

How-To Structure

Although almost always fruitful, the task of developing data for use in a business plan can be very tedious. To help expedite and simplify the process, we present here dozens of exhibits and suggested formats. There is also a sample completed business plan in the Appendix that illustrates many of the concepts and principles discussed throughout the book.

The book is divided into two distinct parts. Chapters 2 through 5 take the reader through the conceptual and data-gathering phases of the business planning process: determining and targeting the audience for the plan; assessing the company's internal and external strengths, weaknesses, opportunities, and threats; setting goals, objectives, and related strategies for the organization. Part Two, Chapters 6 to 11, concentrates on the practical aspects of converting the results of Part One into a focused plan that will motivate and convince both insiders and outsiders. These chapters discuss preparation for plan assembly, the four key sections of the document—organization, sales, production, and finance—and putting together the finished product.

Contemporary Management Techniques

It was not our objective in writing this book to create a dictionary of the hundreds of management and strategic philosophies and techniques that have been on the bestseller racks over the past five years. We did, however, try to provide perspective on what we consider to be the major trends in management thinking as they affect each section of the plan. For instance, the just-in-time (JIT) inventory control method and activity-based costing (ABC) are described in context in Chapter 9. Readers are both admonished and encouraged in this regard: They must be careful not to create a plan too full of modern management theory that may not be understood or trusted by the target audience. But the opportunity to improve the organization should never be allowed to pass them by just because it is new. Change is an essential element in sustaining and growing a business.

Chapter 2
Structuring the Plan in Accordance With Its Use

The objective of this chapter is to describe the practical ways in which the intended use of the business plan should guide its development and content and to present some basic concepts and major uses of business planning. These uses may include internal management and planning activities as well as external presentation for financing or divestiture. The users of the business plan will have significantly different interests and needs. Therefore, the content and emphasis of the business plan should satisfy these needs and provide the information necessary for decision and action to be taken. For example, a business plan intended for bank financing of cash flow would emphasize the predictability of sales and expenses, whereas one for capital expansion might emphasize the impact of capital equipment on existing production and earnings capacity.

Regardless of its use, there are several key components to a good business plan. It should present the business concept and market clearly and succinctly. It should describe the strategy and method of competition the company will use to meet customer needs effectively and to remain competitive. It should also describe existing human and technological resources and the method of organizing and coordinating the production of goods and services. Finally, a good business plan should be consistent and realistic, taking into consideration the current state of the company and the business challenges it faces.

What Is a Business Plan?

Most readers of this book have had some exposure to business planning. In business school, lack of planning has become a routinely cited explanation for the business failures describes in case studies. Outside of academia, business planning has achieved something of the mystique of motherhood and apple pie. But practically, the challenge is to apply planning concepts not in a historical or conceptual context but in a pragmatic way that will set direction and coordinate all resources toward that direction.

An effective plan may be presented through a planning document, but the business plan itself should be a set of management decisions about the company's desired and intended course of action. In its most basic form, business planning is the process of deciding what the company will do to be successful, what method of competition it will use, and the specific actions that are required.

The scope and complexity of the process and resulting plan will obviously depend on the nature and status of the company. Smaller companies may be able to identify a desired course of action in a single meeting of principals, perhaps at a retreat setting once each year. By contrast, a larger company in a more unpredictable business market may need a more structured and complex planning process, if only to collect and analyze the information required to make strategic decisions.

Finally, the various audiences of business planning may include, in addition to the company's owners and work force, the customers, suppliers, and community at large—especially in the case of companies facing restructuring to avoid ultimate business failure. Beyond sustained economic viability, each of these audiences looks to the company for something different. Most in turn must base their own business and personal plans on their understanding of those of the company.

A formula approach to life does not work; nor can a formula be comprehensively applied to a company's business planning. For this reason, we shall focus on the application of concepts and techniques that result in a comprehensive and integrated business plan unique to each company.

What Are the Objectives and Uses of a Business Plan?

A good business plan not only describes the direction of the company, but also provides the logic, rationale, and mechanics underlying that direction. This supporting information allows internal and external users to decide on or modify their own courses of action. For example, a desired and necessary expansion of the production facility may require external capital, which in turn requires bank support. However, it may also involve relocation, which influences the desirability of existing workers being transferred to a new location.

The premise of this book is that it is both desirable and possible to plan an integrated and comprehensive direction for any company. However, it may not be practical, desirable, or necessary to describe that direction at length in a formal written document. Given the divergent interests of the various audiences who will use the business plan, it is better to tailor any written presentation to the specific needs of the intended user and to choose the form and detail that will most effectively communicate the appropriate information.

There are five primary situations that may require a business plan. Each situation involves different users of business plan information, each with different interests and objectives. They include:

Business Plan Situation	Business Plan Users	
1. Internal planning and forecasting	Internal	
2. Obtaining funding for ongoing operations	External and internal	
3. Obtaining funding for expansion	External and internal	
4. Divestiture, acquisition, or spin-off	External or internal	
5. Restructuring or reorganization	External or internal	

We now describe each of the major uses of plans, the interests of the users, and the emphasis of the business plan in different situations.

Internal Planning and Forecasting

One primary use of the business plan is to coordinate resources and activities, particularly across functional or divisional boundaries. The users of this information ideally include everyone in the company. Upper management will use the information to gauge the desirability of performance thresholds for major initiatives, presumably within the context of the company's existing capacity and capabilities. Divisional and functional managers will use the information to guide ongoing production and operational decisions, including the tie to performance management for personnel. Finally, the work force will use the information to align its own performance and reward expectations with the overall company direction. Any lack of these internal linkages will limit the ability of the company to consistently implement its strategic initiatives and will also limit its longer-term competitive potential. It is surprising to find that management and workers often make well-intentioned decisions that are in fact dysfunctional simply because they do not understand how the company's basic business plan translates into their daily sphere of activity.

The business plan is particularly important in personnel planning and development. The human resource function of the company must anticipate the staffing requirements that the plan dictates, both in numbers and skills. The timing of acquiring these skills must dovetail with the needs of the company, since significant lead time may be necessary to acquire scarce skills or the required numbers within certain economic constraints. Personnel promotion and retraining requirements must also be anticipated to provide career path alternatives while sustaining a work force with a growing set of skills.

The business plan for internal planning and forecasting should emphasize:

- Clear communication of the business concept and strategy
- Integration of functional goals with company objectives
- Detailed description of the process for implementation
- Contingency plans to guide the direction if hurdles or deadlines are not met
- Capability to translate the plan into capital and operational budgets

The most effective business plan for internal planning and forecasting use includes the documentation needed by owners, managers, and the work force. However, it makes its impact when the work force understands how to make decisions that consistently support company strategy. This aspect of strategic guidance and coordination often provides the competitive difference between organizations that are otherwise comparable.

Obtaining Funding Support for Ongoing Operations

Outside banking and investment firms typically need business plan materials to enable them to analyze the feasibility of the requested funding support to meet the company's cash flow requirements. This financial support may be tied to the financial performance of the company, especially if the lending limits are determined or collateralized by specific asset values. The more active and reputable funding sources receive funding requests and business plans in volume, often without prior contact or solicitation. Therefore, a concise but thorough presentation must convey the results of the planning process as it regards the need for funding. The primary concern of these funding sources is the predictability and timing of cash flow, but the business plan must also address the overall viability of the company and give a prognosis as to how it will perform in the current competitive climate.

The business plan for obtaining funding for ongoing operations should emphasize:

- The predictability of cash flow
- Debt coverage provided from cash flow
- Purpose of and need for cash flow funding
- The financial management expertise within the company
- Type and value of assets to be used to collateralize debt
- The capital and ownership structure of the company

The interest or lack of interest of funding sources depends on their assessment of the lending risk and the potential return involved. The criteria applied in their analysis will be unique to their own business objectives. However, their attention will focus on the credibility of the financial presentations they receive.

Obtaining Funding for Expansion

Business expansion includes start-up activities as well as entry into new markets, new product development, and construction or acquisition of a major facility. Funding sources for expansion typically differ from those providing cash flow lending. The cash needed for a significant expansion may require equity as well as debt sources of cash. Collateral may be a major consideration in equipment-based lending or leasing, because the risk to the lender will be evaluated on the basis of the future value of the equipment and the business, both valued from the perspective of sustained earnings capacity. The economics of the industry is a significant consideration of the expansion lender or investor, because without a viable market the value of the business and of any specialized production equipment will of necessity be impaired.

The debt or equity investor will also look to the tangible values of the assets and to the potential for unexpected changes in technology or competition that could affect the credibility of the plan's key assumptions. In determining feasibility from a presentation, these investors will attempt to substantiate or refute assumptions that underlie and support the anticipated financial outcomes. This process of due diligence will initially focus on the written presentation but may also include independent verification of critical facts. At any point in the due diligence process, facts that are inconsistent with the statements and assumptions of the plan will impair its overall credibility.

The business plan for obtaining funding for business expansion should emphasize:

- Scope of the market and overall profit potential
- Relevant management and technical experience of key personnel
- Initial and liquidation value of assets to be used as collateral
- Debt service and collateral coverage
- Return on investment potential (if an equity investment)
- Risk factors and contingency plans to address them

Expansion financing requires assurance that the capital structure of the company can support the debt leverage proposed. Risk and performance issues must be resolved or made thoroughly understandable by the information given in the business plan.

Divestiture, Acquisition, or Spin-Off

The business plan is typically the primary source of information available to potential buyers of the company. It is unlikely that any potential buyer will be able to understand all the intricacies of the company and its industry prior to assuming operational control. However, the buyer must understand and accept the basic business premise underlying the company in order to invest money and energy. For this reason, potential buyers look for indications of the long-term viability of the company through its competitive or strategic positioning in its market. However, few companies can realize the potential of their market without a trained work force and adequate production capacity.

The primary interest of a buyer is in the strengths and weakness of the company's basic functional components and in the management capability that ties them together. A business plan prepared for the purposes of divestiture, merger, or joint venture must present the strengths of the business and also describe plans to overcome any weaknesses. In the case of a basically viable company, the buyer may consider the realistic potential for continuity of the basic business. In the case of a troubled company or new venture, the buyer may more closely analyze the amount of time and effort necessary to keep it afloat and the likelihood that required outcomes will be achieved. One common and often erroneous premise underlying business combinations is that a tangible synergy will result. The potential for realizing this synergy is commonly assumed but not adequately managed, with the result that performance is often below the threshold required for feasibility.

The business plan used for the spin-off of a product line or division of the company is a hybrid of all other forms of business plans but is most similar to a plan for divestiture. The existing business unit must be definable as a new business entity, typically requiring new business functions, such as accounting and finance, that were previously performed by the parent company. In many cases, the buyer may be existing management or an investor group. Their interests will be similar to those of investors in an acquisition.

Plans to acquire or expand a product line typically require an analysis of feasibility and economics, as well as of production and distribution logistics. The business plan for the introduction or expansion of a product line typically focuses on the product line both as a strategic business unit and as an enterprise supported by a wide variety of corporate functions. Plans and requirements may mirror the business plan topics for the entire company but provide greater detail on production costs, distribution logistics, and timing. Corporate support functions may be described only in terms of the extent required for the product line and the associated corporate allocation of overhead.

The business plan for acquisition, divestiture, or spin-off should emphasize:

- The potential for improvements in profitability and market share
- The competitive position and advantages of the company
- The synergy potential in related or complementary industries or companies
- The key managerial and technical skills within the company
- The financial capacity of the company to cover the debt service funding the acquisition while providing an acceptable rate of return

Capital markets uses require verifiable factual information. Inconsistent information may cause significant problems during due diligence and negotiations.

Restructuring or Reorganization

The business plan may be the action agenda to restore profitability or production capacity. This agenda may be required by outside parties, either lenders requiring financial viability or buyers wanting to merge operations into another business form. The primary focus of this type of business plan is on identifying operational changes that will reduce production, distribution, and administrative expenses. This form of business plan typically focuses on performance and operational measures that require major adjustments in one or more functional aspects of the company. Elimination of

tion lot sizes; lead times for acquiring materials and scarce skills; and programs to ensure quality consistent with the value objectives for each product.

3. *Research and product development strategy*—including the development of new products and introduction of new technology; decisions on product life-cycle reengineering or replacement; and methods to keep up with outside technical developments.

4. *Organization and management strategy*—including determining the economic feasibility of the business through identification of funding requirements; procedures to ensure adequate controls over assets and access to key management, supervisory, and production talent; and methods to effectively coordinate long-range company objectives and strategy and translate them into day-to-day tactics and operations.

5. *Financial performance strategy*—including the financial ability to fund the cash requirements of the company, motivate and reward the work force, justify investment through acceptable rates of return on investment, support lending for debt requirements, and sustain the competitiveness of the company.

These strategic issues form the core of any comprehensive business plan.

How Should the Planning Process Be Organized?

An implicit requisite for the development of an effective business plan is an interactive, multidisciplinary process. Team effort is an absolute must for such a significant undertaking. The creativity of each functional area in the company must be tapped, because the success of the plan will depend on consistent implementation at the functional level. Also, most of the company's technical skills usually reside within the functions, including product development, production engineering, distribution and sales efforts, financial analysis, and human resources.

While each company should create a planning process that meets its specific needs and circumstances, a consistent set of iterative steps should generally be followed. The remainder of this chapter describes one planning sequence that could be followed.

Steps in the Planning Sequence

1. *Organize the planning process.* Top management must first identify the parties to be involved, outline the basic scope of the planning process, and decide on the time frame for its completion. In some cases, outside parties may also be involved, either to provide technical input or to facilitate some other aspect of the planning sessions. Top management's commitment to the planning process must be communicated to all participants and then reinforced. The responsibilities of each party should be defined.

A work plan should be prepared to supplement the general timetable and to ensure adequate time for all areas of planning. Some aspects of the planning process will require extensive data analysis and perhaps research efforts by staff members. One technique is to work backward in developing the work plan and timetable, starting with the due dates of major milestones to determine by when each step and activity involved in those milestones must be completed.

In some situations, such as financing for an acquisition, the timetable for developing a plan may be dramatically shortened. In these circumstances, it may be best to identify the information required from each participant, meet to develop the plan concepts in a location away from distractions, and attempt to bring to completion only those plan components required for the special purpose. It is much easier to develop materials for a special-purpose plan when the company can work from an overall plan that is in place. Many companies find that it is easier to keep the planning process ongoing than to attempt to create special-purpose planning documents without this background information.

Teamwork is another dimension of planning that is beneficial to the planning process. The overall purpose of the process should be to integrate the functional activities of the company so that they are directed toward consistent objectives. In this regard, it may be useful to have managers work together in collecting and analyzing data prior to presentation and discussion in a formal planning session. Also, specific data needs identified during the development of the plan may be assigned for routine collection and analysis during the course of normal operations. The planning group may be able to redefine the information needed to direct the company toward the performance goals identified in the plan.

2. *Assess the company's internal operating environment and capabilities.* This evaluation should identify the strategic strengths and weaknesses of each function in the business. Also, the adequacy of the management structure should be assessed. The process for internal assessment is described in detail in Chapter 3.

3. *Assess the company's external environment.* This step involves evaluating such outside factors as the economy, the competition, technological advances, regulatory issues, and related factors that may be influenced by but not controlled by the company. It is particularly important to consider current circumstances as well as trends and future developments that could have an impact on the environment. From this analysis, a better understanding of the company's internal capabilities and its need for change and adaptation can be developed. The process for assessing the external environment is described in detail in Chapter 4.

4. *Define strategy and set goals.* This step involves using one's understanding of the internal and external environments to define a fundamental strategy for the business. The strategy should define the method of competition that the company will use to be successful in its environment. In turn, the method of competition helps to determine the form of organization, the market focus, and the philosophy of serving the company's customers. From this strategy, performance and operational goals can be identified for functional areas of the business as well as for the company in general. These goals must be realistic, given the time and resources necessary to create the

required operational capabilities. The process for developing the strategy and setting goals is described in detail in Chapter 5.

5. *Prepare for plan assembly.* This step involves translating the overall strategy and goals into specific plans and programs. While goals define the operating and performance objectives, plans and programs provide the direction for managing the company's resources. This step is particularly important because it requires pragmatic efforts to change the daily activities and priorities of the business to support a redefined set of objectives and standards. At this point, theory becomes practice as the company moves from strategy toward action. The process for preparing the plan materials for integration and assembly is described in detail in Chapter 6.

6. *Develop an organizational plan.* Identifying the form of organization and the organizational characteristics necessary to accomplish the goals of the company is the next step. The organizational plan should include the organization and management structure as well as the management and control systems that support the structure. In addition, the cost and organizational requirements for supporting this structure must be budgeted. The process for developing an organizational plan is described in detail in Chapter 7.

7. *Develop a sales plan.* This step, basically, involves deciding on the methods and activities that will best accomplish the revenue goals of the company. The sales plan must identify the customer base, the products to be sold, the marketing and sales programs to follow, the methods of distribution, and the pricing to achieve the gross margin goals. Because sales drives the other functional activities of the company, a range of revenue outcomes should be presented so that the production and financial plans can develop contingencies to address a range of revenue outcomes. The cost and organizational requirements for the sales effort, distribution strategy, and marketing program must be budgeted. The process for developing a sales plan is described in detail in Chapter 8.

8. *Develop a production plan.* A production plan should describe the production technology, capacity, and scheduling requirements for a given manufacturing facility. This plan should be based on the sales plan and describe the range of production options that are available to produce the required mix and quantity of products. From this, detailed plans for all production resources, including labor, materials, production supervision, and indirect production expenses, can be budgeted. The methods of accounting for production costs must be identified and applied to develop a cost-of-goods-sold budget range for each major product group. The cost-of-goods-sold and pricing analysis must be refined to determine the actions needed to meet the gross margin requirements of the company. The process for developing a production plan is described in detail in Chapter 9.

9. *Develop a financial plan.* This step involves developing prospective financial information that details the financial implications of the organizational, sales, and production plans. The initial set of presentations should describe the financing and cash flow requirements that result from various operating scenarios. From this analysis,

organizational, sales, and production plans may have to be modified to support the realistic constraints of funding, either from internal cash sources or outside cash infusion. Typically, the financial presentation includes projections of income, balance, and cash flow. The process of budgeting and financial control should also be described. The process for developing a financial plan is described in detail in Chapter 10.

      10. *Assemble the completed business plan.* The final step in the planning process is to pull together the information and iterative analysis of all the plans into a final business plan. Working schedules should be prepared for distribution and use, and a final written document may be prepared to reflect the results of the planning process. The process for assembling the completed business plan is described in detail in Chapter 11.

Not Just for Manufacturers

For purposes of consistent illustration, the examples we present in this study assume a manufacturing company that produces a physical product for distribution and sale. Unique considerations for other types of companies, including distribution and service organizations, are noted. The illustrative examples are relevant to companies that do not produce a physical product if they consider their client service personnel to be an inventory of service capacity that depends on the service technology used in generating revenue. Just as production equipment can produce a specified set of goods within a period of time, so can service industry workers produce a specified set of services, or service units, within a period of time. The logistics of planning either production capacity or service capacity are similar in all but name. In this regard, the techniques described in this book are directly applicable to service and distribution industries. Business plan presentations to outside investors and funding sources will be scrutinized in a similar manner.

      Without adequate consideration, planning may not produce the desired results. Therefore, it is worth highlighting some overall suggestions for the planning process. Here are five:

1. Commitment by top management to the planning process and the final results projected is a requirement. Outside and internal audiences will both have an interest in seeing the plan implemented or modified when circumstances change.
2. Both short- and longer-term objectives and strategies should be addressed so that the company is directed to action that is neither shortsighted nor unrealistic.
3. Inadequacies identified during the planning process, particularly in the availability of information or understanding of the competitive environment, should be resolved through operational changes.
4. Ideally the plan should be as simple and understandable as possible. Nearly

everyone working for the company should be able to describe how their work and objectives support the overall strategies identified in the plan.
5. The plan should include contingencies that will allow the company to adapt to actual results while remaining focused on the strategic objectives set forth in the plan.

An effective plan should be integrated into operations so that periodic updates become part of annual goal and budget setting. A business plan that is not integrated into operational planning and budgeting will not be effective. Conversely, a business plan that is integrated into operations can be revised when circumstances and critical assumptions change.

Chapter 3
Assessing a Company's Internal Operating Environment and Capabilities

An understanding of the structure and character of the company's internal operating environment is a prerequisite to planning for sustained performance. This understanding allows the company to zero in on factors that affect performance.

The purpose of assessing the internal operating environment is to identify the strengths and weaknesses of the company as well as threats to the organization and opportunities it might exploit.

Important factors shaping the company's operating environment are the nature of its production and the structure of its business operations. Key issues in this regard are:

- The determination of products and services the company provides
- The customers and market segments the company markets to
- The competitive dimensions on which the company chooses to compete
- The values, objectives, and perceptions of owners regarding growth, expansion, and business risk
- The methods and techniques used to define, stimulate, and evaluate performance

Decisions on these issues provide a framework for the way the company conducts its business. This framework allows the company to compare itself with its competitors and orient its operations to the needs of its customers.

The Components and Structure of an Internal Assessment

A commonly used assessment technique is a SWOT analysis, that is, an evaluation of the company's *Strengths*, *Weaknesses*, *Opportunities*, and *Threats*. The first two are internal references dealing with the strengths of the company—its products, production, and management—and weaknesses in these same areas. These two internal dimensions represent controllable factors that, because they can be affected by management action, should therefore be addressed in business planning.

Whether the external analysis should precede the internal analysis is an academic question. The key point is that an effective planning process requires both an internal analysis to identify the company's strengths and weaknesses and an external analysis to identify where the opportunities and threats lie. In practice, both these analyses should be ongoing and concurrent activities.

Here, we first address the internal analysis. For most small to medium-size companies, this is the most feasible aspect of the evaluation process and the one that yields the most valuable information about factors affecting the company's competitive position. Why should this be so?

- Many small to medium-size companies are in market structures in which market position is not strongly affected by rapidly changing technological advances or customer tastes.
- Many small to medium-size companies are in markets where the action of any single competitor will not dramatically affect the entire market.
- Comprehensive, sophisticated external analyses are beyond the capabilities and resources of most small to medium-size companies.
- An internal assessment typically yields some useful insights into marketplace developments, which can then become priority areas for investigation in the external assessment.
- An internal assessment provides a framework for evaluating the significance of external developments and their potential impact on the company's competitive position and future performance.

An external assessment takes on larger importance as an increasing number of competitive factors and market variables affect the company's competitive position. This is also true when the company's market tends toward instability.

Throughout this chapter, and in later chapters as well, we offer various exhibits as sample methods of collecting and analyzing data. But they are not the only methods and should not stifle the reader's creativity in developing other forms of analysis. In the area of business planning, knowledge is truly power; the more you know, the better the decision-planning process.

The purpose of assessing the internal capabilities of the company is to obtain a concise, focused understanding of its strengths and weaknesses and their effect on its ability to grow, to be profitable, and to remain economically viable. The focus of an internal assessment is to evaluate the effectiveness and the financial impact of the business strategies that the company is currently following. Therefore, the assessment must address each of the business strategies described here: marketing, production, research and development, organization and management, and financial.

The effectiveness of an internal assessment is enhanced if performance is viewed over a multiyear time period (for instance, two to five years) and key trends are identified. This historical perspective is important to an understanding of cause-and-effect relationships. A review and analysis of historical information for any recent period of time can also provide useful insights, so long as the company recognizes that there may be limitations with restricted time periods.

In the light of these considerations, we describe an approach for completing an evaluation of each business strategy.

Evaluating Market Strategy

The starting point in evaluating market strategy is to determine what the company has been able to sell, to whom, in what quantities, at what price, and with what level of effort. Therefore, the focal questions of the analysis become:

- Who are and have been our key customers?
- What products or services have they purchased?
- What has been the level of their purchases?
- How has the level of purchase been affected by product prices, promotion, and distribution policies and efforts?
- What has been the net impact on revenue levels of changes in product or service prices?

These questions can be answered by using data from the company's accounting system and sales records to complete a historical trend analysis. An analysis of key customer sales, a product revenue analysis, and a geographic sales analysis should be completed as part of this analysis.

Key Customer Sales Analysis

Exhibit 3-1 provides a format for an annual comparative summary of sales for key customers over a five-year period. The number of customers included in the analysis should provide a broad representation of sales by product type. The economist Vilfredo Pareto noted that in most cases relatively few customers account for a significant portion of business volume. The rule of thumb that follows is that 80 percent of the company's revenues come from 20 percent of its customers. The point is to analyze a large enough portion of the revenue base to draw meaningful inferences from the results.

The purpose of the analyses is to spot trends and anomalies that may affect or

Exhibit 3-1. Key customer sales analysis.

Customer	Year						5-Yr. % Change
	1	2	3	4	5		
1 Customer A Sales revenue Revenue/order							
2 Customer B Sales revenue Revenue/order							
3 Customer C Sales revenue Revenue/order							
4 Customer D Sales revenue Revenue/order							
5 Customer E Sales revenue Revenue/order							
n Customer n Sales revenue Revenue/order							
Total Customer 1 through n Total Company Sales							

help to define the business plan. Collectively, they may yield significant insights into how the company is doing. For instance, a steady decline in customer order size, combined with a decrease in sales for a particular product, may pinpoint a specific problem in product quality, delivery, or service.

Among the analyses that could be performed are the following:

1. *Has volume per customer increased or decreased?* How can this be explained? Is this good or bad? Does the company rely extensively on one customer or customer group? (Higher volume may mean lower sales and handling costs per dollar of revenue.)
2. *Has the customer base been retained?* If not, what explains the turnover? Is the customer base expanding? (High turnover may indicate quality or service problems.)

3. *Has the average order size been increasing or decreasing?* Smaller average order size may indicate changes in customer buying patterns or in price competition.
4. *Has the frequency of orders changed?* Are customers adopting just-in-time purchasing policies? Or are they expanding the number of sources from which they purchase goods?

An assessment of the contribution of each customer to the company's growth can frequently be enlightening. Revenue per order is generally a valid indicator of the amount of effort required to generate a level of sales and of the potential to generate additional sales revenue from the customer. This assumes that each order entails sales and promotion, processing, and distribution costs. The revenue-per-order ratio provides an indication of the leverage of sales and promotion efforts.

The key customer sales analysis can be completed on the basis of individual customers, but it should also include definable customer segments. These segments can be defined in terms of industry sectors, end-use products or services, or purchasing objectives. It may not be appropriate at this point to define customer segments in terms of geography, because the purpose of the analysis is to discern how much and why customers buy, not where they buy.

Product Revenue Analysis

Doing an analysis like that shown in Exhibit 3-2 is critical for understanding the value of the company's production and its market potential. It is the basis for determining if the current mix of products and services can yield sufficient revenue—both now and in the future—or if adjustments to the mix are appropriate or even necessary. The basic input for this analysis is product and product group sales by units and dollars for each of the most recent years.

Product revenue analysis provides an annual comparative summary of sales volume and revenue levels for each of the company's key products or service lines. For each product, the analysis provides a five-year history of the average unit price. The sales volume is the number of units of the product or service sold during the year times the average unit price. Trends in unit volume indicate the extent to which demand is growing, stagnating, or declining. Trends in sales revenue per unit describe changes in pricing, production costs, or raw material costs.

These trends provide some insight into the company's product lines. First, the relationship between changes in unit price and changes in sales revenue gives some indication of the elasticity of demand for the product or service. Product demand elasticity, in simple terms, describes the impact of price increases or decreases on the total revenue generated by a specific product. For example, a price increase may be desirable if it has a net positive impact on sales dollars, even though it has a negative impact on the number of units sold. In this case, the additional revenue on the sale of each unit resulting from the price increase more than compensates for the loss of revenue from diminished unit volume. This suggests that sales of a product may be strongly affected by factors other than price. Similarly, a price decrease is generally

Exhibit 3-2. Product revenue analysis showing a five-year trend.

Revenue Factor	Year					5-Yr. % Change
	1	2	3	4	5	
1 Product A Avg. unit price Annual sales in dollars Revenue/order						
2 Product B Avg. unit price Annual sales in dollars Revenue/order						
3 Product C Avg. unit price Annual sales in dollars Revenue/order						
4 Product D Avg. unit price Annual sales in dollars Revenue/order						
n Product n Avg. unit price Annual sales in dollars Revenue/order						
Company avg. unit price Company avg. Revenue/order						

not desirable unless it increases demand to the point where there is a net positive impact on revenue. Also, a price decrease may not be desirable unless it is necessary to maintain demand and/or market position in response to actions by competitors.

The company must understand the price sensitivity of demand for its products and services. This understanding can be developed only by evaluating the relationship between unit price, product sales, and sales revenue over an extended period of time. The relationship between unit price and changes in sales volume provides some indication of the continuing strength of demand for the product or service. If the unit price has remained fairly stable over the period of analysis, changes in sales volume indicate whether the demand for the company's product is growing, stabilizing, stagnating, or declining.

Additional analyses, such as that shown in Exhibit 3-3, can be helpful in pinpointing the reasons for any trends identified. For example, if the rate of growth has

Exhibit 3-3. Product/customer analysis.

Customer	Products or Services				
	Type A	Type B	Type C	Type D	Type n

Customer A
  Avg. $$ volume
  Increase (+) Decrease (−)					

Customer B
  Avg. $$ volume
  Increase (+) Decrease (−)					

Customer C
  Avg. $$ volume
  Increase (+) Decrease (−)					

Customer D
  Avg. $$ volume
  Increase (+) Decrease (−)					

Customer n
  Avg. $$ volume
  Increase (+) Decrease (−)					

diminished, the general demand for the company's type of product or service may be in plateau or decline, or the demand for the company's specific product may be declining relative to the demand for the products of competitors.

If the unit price has changed over the period of analysis, the relationship between changes in unit price and changes in sales volume is also an indicator of the product's elasticity of demand. If the demand for the product becomes more elastic—that is, more price-sensitive—the underlying strength of demand may remain strong so long as the rate of growth in sales volume is at least stable.

In summary, product revenue analyses are important in: (1) identifying trends in customers and products; (2) assessing the ongoing demand for the company's products or services; (3) determining the significance of price as an influence on demand for the products or services; (4) identifying the increasing or decreasing significance of individual products or services as contributors to the company's overall revenue; and (5) identifying priority areas for investigation in the external assessment.

Geographic Sales Analysis

Exhibit 3-4 provides a format for an annual comparative summary of sales volume, revenue levels, and related sales and marketing expenses for the major geographic

Area	Year					5-Yr. % Change
	1	2	3	4	5	
1 Area 1						
Sales in units						
Sales dollars						
Direct selling						
Promotion, advertising						
Distribution						
Revenue/expense ratio						
2 Area 2						
Sales in units						
Sales dollars						
Direct selling						
Promotion, advertising						
Distribution						
Revenue/expense ratio						
n* Area *n						
Sales in units						
Sales dollars						
Direct selling						
Promotion, advertising						
Distribution						
Revenue/expense ratio						
Company Totals						

Exhibit 3-4. Geographic sales analysis.

areas served by the company. In order to complete this analysis, data by product and by region for sales revenue, sales and marketing expenses, and distribution costs must be available. Obviously this analysis can and should be performed by taking various cuts of the data, for instance, product/product lines within geographic regions.

The purpose of the geographic sales analysis is to determine the fundamental relationships between marketing and sales expenses and the revenues resulting from marketing and sales efforts. The company must decide if the revenue history and potential of certain markets justifies the costs of continuing to serve them.

The focal point of the analysis is the revenue-to-expense ratio. The ratio should, of course, exceed 1.0 by a considerable margin. However, there may be strategic reasons why it does not. For example, the start-up of a new market segment or distribution channel may require significant funding during introduction. If there is a wide disparity in the value of the ratios across geographical areas, the company must decide either to concentrate its efforts on expanding demand and sales in high-payoff areas or to identify and implement more productive and cost-effective marketing and sales strategies in low-payoff areas.

The geographic sales analysis may be expanded beyond geographic parameters. It could be completed on whatever basis the company has organized its sales force, promotion efforts, and distribution system. For example, some companies organize their sales and distribution activities on the basis of product lines or customer segments rather than geographical areas. The objective is to be able to relate these costs to the resulting sales revenues and obtain an understanding of the relative leverage and payoff from sales expenditures and programs.

The results of the key customer sales, the product revenue, and the geographic sales analyses provide information about the strengths, weaknesses, and trends in the company's market strategy. If the company's sales are concentrated in only one or a few geographical areas, the geographic sales analysis becomes less important. By the same token, if the company's sales are concentrated among a few customer segments, the key customer sales analysis becomes more important. The questions to consider as a result of evaluating the market strategy are:

- What are the trends in each sales segment?
- What are the characteristics of customers who are the primary sources of unit sales? Of revenues? Is the company overly dependent on certain customers or customer segments? Are traditional sources of sales and revenues declining? What groups of products or services are growing? Which are strategic and competitive?
- What are the emerging relationships between sales volume and sales revenue for the company's major product/service lines? Is there any indication of pressure on prices or price flexibility?
- How is market demand influencing the historical mix of products? Which products are growing, plateauing, stagnating, or declining?
- How effective is the company's marketing and sales organization in leveraging expenditures for sales of higher-margin strategic products?

The answers to these questions are the basis for developing a fairly complete profile of the strengths of a market strategy, on which the company should build—and its weaknesses, which the company will either eliminate or strive to correct.

In addition to these basic analyses, there are many more detailed analyses of the market strategy that a company can undertake if its accounting and records systems can produce the necessary data.

Evaluating Production Strategy

An evaluation of market strategy focuses on the revenue-generating potential of the company. An evaluation of production strategy concentrates to a great extent on its cost-control and technical capabilities. In this evaluation, the company must address all of the factors that affect production and service costs and identify the trends in and relationships among these factors. Several of the key factors are the costs of raw materials and supplied products/services, labor and technical availability, and labor productivity. An analysis of these factors, their impact on overall production costs, and the potential for more cost-effective methods is critical in determining the effectiveness of the company's competitive strategy.

The focal point of the analysis is to determine:

1. *Which raw materials and supplied products/services are critical to the production process?* Who supplies them? Are any supplier relationships critical to the company? What impact would cost increases in raw materials or supplied products/services have on the company?
2. *What are labor costs in terms of wages and fringe benefits?* What is the extent of technical leverage provided by the production equipment and processes? What is the productivity obtained from the labor force?
3. *What are the company's costs for space and equipment?* What are the capacity and productivity rates of its equipment, as used both currently and potentially? What are the historical and potential relationships between production volume, equipment productivity, and labor productivity?
4. *Does the company produce within defined quality standards?* How does the production process ensure compliance with the quality objectives set by the company and its customers?

The company can answer many of these questions by calling up data from its production and cost accounting systems. The topic of quality assurance will be discussed in greater detail in Chapter 7.

In evaluating its production strategy, the company should distinguish between the overall factors that are *common* among products and those that are *unique* to specific products. The company should recognize that the ultimate objective of this assessment is to understand its standard production costs. These costs must be known in advance of preparing the production operating plan. Four aspects of analysis are necessary in this assessment.

Overall Labor Costs Analysis

Exhibit 3-5 is a format for an annual comparative summary of cost and productivity data for each major class of worker. Productivity assessment must be based on productivity measures and data such as completed units per worker hour and value added per labor dollar. Worker classes should be defined on the basis of existing or trainable skills, tasks performed, products produced, or some similar measure of comparability. For each worker class, the analysis requires data from four areas of information. First, the average unit cost must be split into two major components of labor costs—wages and fringe benefits. (Benefits should be defined to include support

Exhibit 3-5. Labor cost analysis.

Cost Factor	Year					5-Yr. % Change
	1	2	3	4	5	
1 *Worker Class A*						
Total avg. unit cost						
Wages						
Fringe benefits						
Number of staff						
Productivity/output per worker						
Supervisor/worker ratio						
Total labor cost						
2 *Worker Class B*						
3 *Worker Class C*						
n *Worker Class n*						

services and benefits provided by the company.) These costs, over a three- to five-year period, indicate the trend in average costs per worker. Second, the number of staff within specific worker classes indicates the trends in the composition of the company's work force. Third, the productivity measures indicate the trends in the output per worker, specifically the extent of leverage provided by the company's production process. These key indicators should provide a basis for determining opportunities for improvement.

Labor performance should be defined in terms of the key quantitative indicators used to evaluate and reward employees within specific labor categories. The supervisor-to-direct-labor-cost ratio indicates the trend in the amount of supervision required in the production process. This important indicator may illustrate the need for more effective labor relations, a need for changes in hiring practices, or a need for more effective training of the direct labor force. Because supervision is an indirect cost, the company will want to ensure that the benefits and objectives set for supervisory positions exceed the associated costs.

In general, the analysis of labor costs should identify the extent to which labor requirements, labor costs, and labor productivity are growing or declining in importance within the company. While labor may be declining as a portion of total produc-

Exhibit 3-6. Overall facilities and equipment cost analysis showing a five-year trend.

	Year					
Cost Factor	*1*	*2*	*3*	*4*	*5*	*5-Yr. % Change*
1 Facilities Space—cost/sq. foot Utilities						
2 Capital Equipment						
Unit A Current NBV Annual maintenance $$ of revenue						
Unit B						
Unit *n*						
3 Capacity utilization factor						

tion costs, it may also represent the greatest opportunity for increases in productivity and competitiveness. It is important to determine whether the relationships among the rates of change in certain factors are reasonable. For example, if the rate of change in labor costs exceeds the rate of change in productivity, the probability of an emerging production cost problem is high. On the other hand, it is important to recognize that a reliable and consistent method of measuring labor and production efficiency is necessary before forming this conclusion. Changes in production technology and processes will more effectively leverage labor costs while offsetting overall profitability owing to investment costs. Therefore, this historical analysis should be based on consistent production levels and should consider the effects of equipment investments.

Overall Facilities and Equipment Cost Analysis

Exhibit 3-6 shows an annual comparison of cost and productivity data for production facilities and equipment. Three major pieces of information are needed annually for the three- to five-year period. First, the total facilities cost must be separated into cost of space and cost of utilities categories. The resulting breakout shows trends in the costs of maintaining and utilizing the production facilities. Next, the costs for capital equipment should be analyzed to determine relevant invested capital (all set at book value), maintenance cost, and revenues produced for each major unit of production equipment. The purpose of looking at net book value (actual cost less accumulated depreciation) is to understand the rate of investment and utilization and to determine the relationships of current investment costs to productivity and maintenance costs. Finally, capacity utilization, which is the relationship between actual production and potential production, should be quantified. This is useful knowledge when determining the opportunities and potential profitability of resizing the production function.

The analysis of facilities and equipment costs should identify the extent to which facilities and equipment costs, investments, and productivity are increasing or decreasing relative to the overall level of production and profitability of the company.

Supplied Products and Services Cost Analysis

The format shown in Exhibit 3-7 provides annual comparative data for four relevant cost categories: (1) supplied materials for products or services; (2) the company's major suppliers of each key component; (3) the average unit costs to the company for each key component; and (4) the volume of purchases for each component from each supplier. This information can be used to calculate an average annual total materials cost for each product. The information should also be used to assess the pricing patterns of specific suppliers and the extent of the company's dependence on individual suppliers.

It should be apparent from Exhibit 3-7 that, depending on the number of products and key components, this analysis can quickly become unwieldy. The objective of the analysis is to ensure that the company's profitability and viability are not jeopardized by overreliance on certain suppliers or by an increase in supplier prices that the company cannot pass along. Therefore, it is important for the company to manage its relationships with suppliers and to understand how these relationships may affect its profitability. If the company does not have adequate information to complete a supplier cost analysis, it should develop a trend analysis for the total production costs associated with specific products. If the analysis indicates significant increases or rates of increase in costs, then the company should further investigate the trends in the costs of specific supplied materials. This analysis can be streamlined by focusing on major sources of supplies or critical components.

The evaluation of production strategy should ultimately identify the costs of developing products and services that in turn are sold to customers. It may appear that this analysis requires an inordinate amount of detailed information. However, for business planning purposes, it is critically important to understand the cost elements of each product or service. It is surprising to find that many companies base their understanding of costs on general information. Upon detailed analysis, they frequently discover that their assumptions about cost behavior do not accurately reflect reality. These incorrect assumptions are typically perpetuated in pricing and production decisions, resulting in lost profitability.

Exhibit 3-7. Supplied products/services cost analysis format.

Product: _____

Component	Supplier	Year										5-Yr. % Change	
		1		2		3		4		5			
		Price	Volume	Price	Volume	Price	Volume	Price	Volume	Price	Volume	Price	Volume

Contribution Analysis

A contribution analysis by product for all products should be performed. The contribution analysis addresses the profitability that each product or service provides relative to the company's overhead and profit objectives. Product-level contribution is defined as the difference between each product's net sales price and its production cost, that is, the gross margin. A contribution analysis has two significant uses. First, it illustrates the range of the product sales mix. For example, if a significant percentage of the company's sales are low-contribution products, the company is expending relatively large amounts of money on a small payoff. This may be acceptable where higher-volume sales offset the limited margin. However, price and volume volatility may present added risk that must be considered in perpetuating low-margin sales. Obviously, market forces shape the sales environment, but the company must seek to balance its mix of lower- and higher-contribution products to achieve some diversification.

Second, the contribution analysis calculates the break-even point for both the company's business operations and its major product groups. Every company should know this information. Given the contribution margins of its products, the company will be able to determine the minimum sales level required to cover its fixed operating costs.

The contribution analysis also provides the basis for evaluating the extent of integration between the marketing and production strategies. As previously discussed, the marketing and production objectives must support each other and result in an economically viable scale of operation for the company.

In concluding an evaluation of production strategy, the company should note the impact of facilities and transportation costs on overall production costs. There is usually some trade-off between the location, number, and size of production facilities and the distances and transportation costs between the facilities, key sources of supply, and key customer markets. The relationship between these cost factors and the impact on total costs should be carefully monitored and evaluated. In more complex situations, cost minimization and modeling techniques may be appropriate to effectively quantify the requirements and economics of production among several facilities and at differing levels of production. This, of course, is one of the essential functions that can be automated in modern automated manufacturing systems.

Evaluating the Research and Development Strategy

The process for evaluating the R&D strategy depends on the R&D objectives that the company has established—and these are seldom held to consistently. The overall purpose of R&D is to maintain or improve the company's competitive position. The extent of R&D depends on the level of investment that the company obtains from the outside or directs to this purpose from internal sources.

Investments in R&D represent current costs to the company that may produce intangible future benefits, so they should be funded for achieving defined objectives. These objectives may be short-term or long-term. The primary bases for evaluating the R&D strategy are apparent in the following questions:

- Do the company's R&D objectives and activities have strategic significance? Is this investment likely to provide tangible benefits?
- Will R&D investments ultimately pay off and leverage the necessary changes toward higher-margin, sustainable products?
- Are scheduled objectives being met?
- Have the results of post R&D activities justified the level of investment made?
- Are the company's R&D activities appropriate in the light of current marketplace trends and developments?

The answers to these questions describe the relative efficiency, effectiveness, and relevance of R&D activities.

Because of its strategic significance, the R&D strategy is probably best evaluated in both qualitative and quantitative terms. Further, it should be evaluated in the context of the findings from the external assessment by asking and answering the following questions:

- Does the company's R&D strategy support and complement its overall competitive strategy? That is, if the company's competitive goal is to be a leading-edge supplier, is the R&D investment proportionally higher?
- Do the company's current R&D capabilities and plans relate to trends and emerging developments in its competitive external environment?
- What is the company's reputation for innovation and continuous product improvement?
- To what extent has the company been able to maintain or expand its market position by continually introducing new or improved products?

The answers to these questions provide useful insight into the effectiveness of the company's R&D strategy.

Evaluating the Organization and Management Strategy

The evaluation of the market, production, and R&D strategies provides key measurements of the effectiveness of the organization and management strategy. If incremental changes in productivity indicate a diminishing or declining position, this fact may also indicate some deficiency in the organization and management strategy. In addition to productivity measures, other quantitative indicators of strategic effectiveness include staff turnover, staff complaints or grievances, and customer complaints. The quantitative assessments are one aspect of the evaluation of organization and management strategy. Beyond the quantitative assessments, an evaluation of organization and management strategy should include assessment of the company's management. This assessment should address the following issues:

- Clarity of the company's goals, performance objectives, and values
- Effectiveness of the company's organizational structure, assignment of responsibilities, and reporting and accountability relationships
- Adequacy of the company's management and supervision processes
- Efficiency of the company's internal communications
- Level of staff morale, skills, and motivation
- Appropriateness of the company's personnel management policies and procedures
- Extent of equity and fairness in the company's compensation policies
- Objectives and capabilities of the company with regard to quality

Information on these aspects of the company may be obtained through interviews, surveys of staff members, contact with customers, and informal observation. In fact, it is often wise to seek outside assistance in this area of the analysis if the company is performing poorly.

Finally, the evaluation of the organization and management strategy must assess the adequacy and appropriateness of the skills within the company. Several dimensions should be considered in making this assessment:

- The current profile of skills and hiring plans should be consistent with anticipated skill needs.
- The company's procedures and ability to recruit and screen qualified staff should ensure access to critical skills at compensation levels consistent with the economics of the company.
- The company's training programs should effectively develop the new skills that are needed to meet its competitive objectives.
- The company's procedures for measuring, evaluating, and improving performance should stimulate continuous improvements.

In effect, the company must use its personnel program to improve performance at all levels, including clerical, technical, professional, supervisory, and managerial positions. Four key questions that must be addressed in this part of the evaluation are:

1. What areas of skills deficiency and poor or inadequate performance exist within the company?
2. How long have these problems existed? What actions have been taken to correct these problems, and what have been the results?
3. To what extent have hired and promoted staff performed effectively in their positions?
4. What types of formal and informal training are provided? What has been the impact of training on overall job performance?

In short, the company must develop a skills profile that identifies current and future skill needs as well as the means for obtaining needed skills from the outside or through internal development. The appropriate frequency for reassessing staff skills should be influenced by trends in staff turnover, changes in operating procedures and technologies, and growth in staff size.

Quality Management

The company's ability to manage the quality process is critical to success in today's environment, and its approach to quality is obviously an important component. Exhibit 3-8 lists the examination categories for the Malcolm Baldrige award and clearly points to those areas of a company most affected by the quality process.

Exhibit 3-9 shows that there are significant costs associated with an ineffective quality program. On the basis of the data obtained in this part of the assessment, the following questions should be addressed to determine how the company's business plans should evaluate quality issues.

- What is the product defect rate? How does this compare with the industry rate? How should it compare with the defect rate of the company's competitors?
- How much excess and obsolete inventory is identified and written off the company's financial statements? How much is currently on hand relative to total inventory turnover?
- What percentage of shipments have problems of some type?
- What percentage and dollar volume of production involves product rework? How does this compare with industry standards?
- Does order entry, inventory management, production scheduling, or work in process complicate production or cause production delays or bottlenecks?
- Does the information system provide relevant information regarding critical success and performance factors?
- What is the extent of activities that do not add value either to the customer or to the quality of the product?
- How are customer complaints handled? How frequent are complaints? How much of the company's business is currently or potentially from repeat orders?

The answer to these questions may well lead the company to conclude that a more effective quality program can enhance its profitability and market position. Customers almost always have a choice, so the relationship between quality and price for the company's products is typically the determining factor in keeping customers loyal.

Evaluating Financial Strategy

An evaluation of financial strategy must focus on six primary issues: (1) liquidity; (2) asset management; (3) debt management; (4) profitability; (5) cash flow; and

Exhibit 3-8. Malcolm Baldrige National Quality Award examination categories.

1.0 Leadership
    1.1 Senior Executive Leadership
    1.2 Quality Values
    1.3 Management for Quality
    1.4 Public Responsibility

2.0 Information and Analysis
    2.1 Scope and Management of Quality Data and Information
    2.2 Analysis of Quality Data and Information

3.0 Strategic Quality Planning
    3.1 Strategic Quality Planning Process
    3.2 Quality Leadership
    3.3 Quality Priorities

4.0 Human Resources
    4.1 Human Resource Management
    4.2 Employee Involvement
    4.3 Quality Education and Training
    4.4 Employee Recognition and Performance Measurement
    4.5 Employee Well-Being and Morale

5.0 Quality Assurance of Products and Services
    5.1 Design and Introduction of Quality Products and Services
    5.2 Process and Quality Control
    5.3 Continuous Improvement of Processes, Products, and Services
    5.4 Quality Assessment
    5.5 Documentation
    5.6 Quality Assurance, Quality Assessment, and Quality Improvement of Support Services and Business Processes
    5.7 Quality Assurance, Quality Assessment, and Quality Improvement of Suppliers

6.0 Quality Results
    6.1 Quality of Products and Services
    6.2 Comparison of Quality Results
    6.3 Business Process, Operational, and Support Service Quality Improvement
    6.4 Supplier Quality Improvement

7.0 Customer Satisfaction
    7.1 Knowledge of Customer Requirements and Expectations
    7.2 Customer Relationship Management
    7.3 Customer Service Standards
    7.4 Commitment to Customers
    7.5 Complaint Resolution for Quality Improvement
    7.6 Customer Satisfaction Determination
    7.7 Customer Satisfaction Results
    7.8 Customer Satisfaction Comparison

Source: U.S. Department of Commerce.

Exhibit 3-9. Hidden costs of quality.

Commonly Measured Failure Costs	Hidden Failure Costs
Scrap	Engineering time
Rework	Management time
Warranty	Shop and field downtime
	Increased inventory
	Decreased capacity
	Delivery problems
	Lost orders

(6) market value. To evaluate its financial strategy, the company should use data from its basic financial statements—the Income Statement, Balance Sheet, and Cash Flow Summary—to prepare a financial ratio analysis. Exhibit 3-10 illustrates the objectives and components of various financial ratios.

Ratio analysis can be used in several ways. First, the company can obtain industry data (from such sources as Dun & Bradstreet and Robert Morris Associates) describing the comparable ratios for other companies in the same industry. Then it can compare and contrast its ratios with industry averages. This approach has the advantage of providing a frame of reference for comparative analysis. Finally, the company can analyze the trends of specific ratios over time and identify indicators of overall financial performance.

From ratio analysis, the company should be able to answer several relevant questions:

- Does the company's liquidity position support its need for short-term or immediate use of funds?
- To what extent is the company leveraging the return on its assets? Is debt and equity high or low relative to profit and return potential?
- Does the company's debt position support additional debt capacity to fund expansion or reinvestment in new technology? What effect does debt service have on profitability and business risk?
- What impact does the company's investment strategy have on overall profitability?
- How effective is the company's cash-flow management program?

The impact of financial policies and performance on the value of the company's stock is important, particularly if it is publicly owned. The shareholders, who may include employees in an employee stock option plan (ESOP), should be able to distinguish between investments that build or sustain longer-term value and expenditures that do not.

The evaluation of financial strategy should recognize that the company's past and current financial performance will affect its future financial performance and its abil-

Exhibit 3-10. Financial ratio analysis.

Issue	Ratio Indicator	Objective	Components
Liquidity	Current	Short-term financial solvency	$\dfrac{\text{Current assets}}{\text{Current liabilities}}$
	Quick	Ability to pay off short-term obligations	$\dfrac{\text{Current assets-Inventory}}{\text{Current liabilities}}$
Asset management: Appropriate mix and use of assets	Inventory utilization	Appropriate level of inventory as a component of assets	$\dfrac{\text{Cost of goods sold}}{\text{Average inventory}}$
	Fixed asset utilization	Capacity utilization of plant and equipment	$\dfrac{\text{Sales}}{\text{Average net fixed assets}}$
	Total assets utilization	Appropriate level of sales for level of investment in assets	$\dfrac{\text{Sales}}{\text{Average total assets}}$
Debt management: Appropriate leveraging of assets	Debt	Capacity for additional borrowing	$\dfrac{\text{Total debt}}{\text{Total assets}}$
	Times interest earned	Ability to pay current interest (which impacts capacity for additional borrowing)	$\dfrac{\text{EBIT*}}{\text{Interest charges}}$
Profitability	Profit margin on sales	Profit generation of each sales dollar	$\dfrac{\text{Net profit after taxes}}{\text{Sales}}$
	Return on total assets	Combined effect of profit generation from sales and asset utilization	$\dfrac{\text{Net profit after taxes}}{\text{Average total assets}}$
	Return on common equity	Rate of return on stockholders'/ owners'/ investment	$\dfrac{\text{Net profit after taxes}}{\text{Average common equity}}$
Cash flow	Average collection period	Impact of sales, credit, and collection policies on cash flow	$\dfrac{\text{Receivables}}{\text{Annual sales} + 360}$
Market value	Price/earnings	Perceived purchase value of company for each dollar of reported earnings per share of common stock	$\dfrac{\text{Price per common share}}{\text{Earnings per common share}}$
	Price/book	Perceived purchase value of company for each book-valued share of common stock	$\dfrac{\text{Price per common share}}{\text{Book value per common share}}$
		Book value per share = $\dfrac{\text{Stockholders' equity}}{\text{Common shares outstanding}}$	

*Earnings before interest and taxes

ity to achieve marketing, production, R&D, and organization and management goals. Therefore, just as the R&D strategy should be evaluated in terms of the company's ability to respond to marketplace developments, the financial strategy should be evaluated in terms of its ability to support desired goals in marketing, production, R&D, and organization and management.

In summary, an internal assessment addresses each of the major strategies that

Exhibit 3-11. Summary of strengths and weaknesses.

Component/Factor	Strength	Weakness

1. Market strategy
    Market share
    Customer base
    Products/service mix
    Price/revenue
    Promotion
    Sales organization
    Distribution		

2. Production strategy
    Supplier relationships
    Cost of materials and supplies
    Labor productivity
    Plant and equipment productivity
    Plant and equipment capacity and location
    Quality control		

3. Research and Development strategy
    Objectives
    Resources
    Capability
    Productivity
    Promotion
    Sales organization
    Distribution		

4. Organization and Management strategy
    Staff skills
    Management systems
    Environment/climate
    Management productivity
    Plant and equipment capacity and location
    Quality control		

5. Financial Strategy
    Liquidity
    Asset management
    Debt management
    Cash flow management
    Investments
    Profitability
    Distribution		

(continued)

Exhibit 3-11. Summary of strengths and weaknesses.

Component/Factor	Strength	Weakness
6. Overall		

comprise the company's operation: marketing, production, research and development, organization and management, and finance. Although the focal points of analysis may vary, the company must recognize the interrelatedness of the strategies in its overall performance and success. Therefore, the analysis should determine the effectiveness of each strategy and its contribution to the company's overall performance.

Using the Results of an Internal Assessment

As a result of the internal assessment, the company should have a concise list of its strengths and weaknesses. This list is a framework for evaluating the potential impact of external developments on the company's future performance, which is dealt with in Chapter 4, and for developing priority areas for improvement in the company's operations and management.

The identification of strengths and weaknesses should be focused, honest, and objective, concentrating on the key strategies for the company's operations. Exhibit 3-11 presents a structured format for this summary.

Chapter 4
Assessing the External Environment

The company's external environment is defined by several types of factors. The first type is the universe of outsiders with whom the company interacts and who are in a position to influence the company's performance. These include competitors, customers, suppliers, and regulators. The second type consists of the forces or trends that affect the company's competitive position. These forces include demographic trends that affect the composition of the customer base; technological trends that can affect the availability, relevance, usefulness, and cost-effectiveness of specific products and services; economic trends that can affect purchasing behavior; and the relative influence of suppliers and customers. A third type is the basic competitive structure of the industry in which the company operates. The relevant factors here are barriers to entering the industry, particularly for new companies in times of market growth, and barriers that existing companies face in leaving the industry, particularly in times of market decline.

Asking and answering the following questions will help to clarify the nature of a company's operating environment:

- *Who are the company's competitors?* What is the degree of competition? In other words, how many competing companies are there, and what is their relative size and influence on each other? On what basis do these companies compete— price, quality, or service?
- *Who are the company's customers or buyers?* What is their purchasing behavior— for example, the timing and amount of their purchases—and what factors affect their behavior? What is the relative power of customers or buyers vis-à-vis the company on issues such as price, discounts and collections, and product/service capabilities?
- *Who are the company's suppliers (including staff with specialized skills)?* What are their capabilities? What is the relative power of suppliers with regard to price, discounts and collections, and product/service capabilities?

- *What is the potential for the number of competitors to change?* How easy or hard is it for new companies to enter the market or for existing companies to leave?
- *What is the impact of technology on demand for the company's products and services?* What are the demographic trends for the company's customer segments? What is the potential for substitute products and services? Are they available?
- *What opportunities and threats will arise as a result of broad societal trends?* What is the potential impact on the company of such long-term developments as the acceleration and magnitude of the rate of change, the aging of the population, and the evolution of the world economy?
- *In what areas is the company subject to legislative or administrative regulation?* How influential are these areas on the company's business operations and on its ability to control costs and generate revenues?

You must know the answer to these questions in order to prepare a plan that addresses the concerns of potential lenders and investors. With an adequate understanding of its external environment, a company can focus its analysis on those factors that most significantly affect its ability to be successful and that are most subject to change and variability. This will allow the company to develop appropriate business strategies that are based both on the expected benefits of the strategy and on the expected risks associated with the strategy in relation to other elements in the environment.

No company can operate without an effective working relationship with its environment. But neither can it control that environment. A company can in fact control or influence only part of its business sphere. In order to be effective, a company must develop and maintain a system for obtaining relevant external information, manage the information that comes from this system, and have the capability to integrate it in key strategic and organizational decisions.

The Purpose of the External Assessment

An external analysis is often the first step in developing a program to collect and manage external information. It provides a baseline for any process and organizational structure that will provide this information on an ongoing basis. In previous chapters, we emphasized that the successful company must understand the structure of its operating environment. The success of the company is determined by its ability to build on strengths and correct weaknesses. It is also determined by its ability to respond appropriately to external forces. These forces include actions by competitors, demographic trends that affect the preferences of customers, and technological trends that affect the competitive advantage of products and services. In addition, the company must be abler to accommodate economic trends that may affect the utility of its products and services, its cost structure, its financial strategy, and its environment.

External forces may represent either threats to or opportunities for continued success. The purpose of an external assessment is to identify these threats and opportunities and to evaluate their impact on and significance for the company's future.

The external assessment provides background for the business plan, specifically by putting the company's business concepts and practices in perspective with the activities and relationships that the company can influence but not control. Many creative and solid business ideas fail to gain market or funding support because the efforts to create a business around these ideas do not adequately create the customer, supplier, and production synergy necessary for long-term success.

The Components of an External Assessment

The structure of the company's environment and what it needs to know about that environment determine the form and objectives of an external assessment. Three components typically included are market dynamics, technological trends, and economic dependencies.

Analysis of Market Dynamics

Market dynamics describe the factors that affect the company's ability to sell its products for profit. These factors include growth and access to market segments, product features and benefits, and price sensitivity.

One critical market force is the market segmentation of the customer base. Purchasing habits and preferences vary among different demographic groups based on their age, sex, race, and other characteristics. Similarly, socioeconomic characteristics, such as education and income, influence purchasing capacity just as preferences do. The company must understand the composition of its customer base, specifically the ultimate users of its products. It must determine how demographic and socioeconomic trends influence its customer base and the corresponding demand for products and features. Data on demographic and socioeconomic characteristics are available from census, government planning, economic development, and chamber of commerce sources. At the first level of analysis, the company must identify the relevant demographic and socioeconomic influences on its customer segments.

A demographic and socioeconomic analysis is also relevant for companies that are predominantly suppliers of goods or services to other companies. The analysis should extend to the end-user customer segments of the company's customers. For example, if the company supplies materials, products, or services to swimming pool manufacturers, the relevant customer segment is the buyer of swimming pools.

The potential impact of external trends on future sales can be assessed by correlating historical sales trends with purchasing trends among key customer segments. For example, if the company has five years of data on sales to key customers and can obtain five-year data on population characteristics or industry sales, it can relate the rates of change to each other. Data are available from local and state planning agencies as well as from industry-specific sources, including the U.S. Department of Commerce, trade associations, and the Robert Morris customer profiles. Any correlation of industry and market trends should be based on forecasts of population size and characteristics or on specific industry trends. It can also be based on an extrapolation of historical trends if there is no other source of prospective information.

In some cases, companies that supply other companies may be able to provide an analysis of trends in sales and revenues within specific industry segments. A company that uses industry sales and revenue trends as the basis for its analysis should be aware of relevant and unrelated factors that influence these sales and revenues. However, demographic, socioeconomic, and industry trends are not always adequate indicators of continuing or future demand. Most products and services are provided and purchased in a "dynamic mode." This means that more companies are likely to enter the market when the demand outlook is favorable. If the demand outlook is poor, some of the company's existing competitors may leave the market. This does not mean that a diminished demand will automatically result in a weaker market position or that sales will decline for a specific company. In addition to potential new entrants, the company's existing competitors may try to capture an increasing share of the existing demand.

Market forces also define the life-cycle stage of specific products and services. Most products and services go through stages in which the rate of sales growth increases, plateaus, and eventually declines. This basic life-cycle pattern is illustrated in Exhibit 4-1. The typical life-cycle pattern is a curve representing four stages: introduction, growth, maturity, and decline. This pattern is illustrated in Graph A. The rate at which a product or service moves through the pattern, and the length of time it spends in any one phase, are influenced by demand, availability of competing or substitute products, and the company's own promotion and product modification efforts.

The potential impact of additional or intensified promotional efforts is reflected in the cycle-recycle pattern illustrated in Graph B. As the rate of growth decreases, the company should attempt to spur additional demand through expanded promotion, product enhancement, or more aggressive pricing efforts. The second cycle of demand eventually reaches maturity and decline, typically in a shorter period of time than the first cycle took. The potential impact of ongoing efforts to find new sources of demand or new uses for existing products is reflected in the scalloped pattern in Graph C. This pattern indicates that the company has penetrated additional customer sales segments or geographic areas, or that the company and its customers have been able to modify the product to obtain additional utility.

The implication of a product's life cycle is that the company must determine and manage the life-cycle stages of each product and service it offers. This, in conjunction with the analysis of the impact of other market forces, assists the company in evaluating the adequacy of its market and product differentiation. The stability of growth and profitability within the company will be enhanced when the life-cycle stages of various products are managed as a portfolio.

A third market force is the position and capabilities of competitors including their entry into or exit from the market. To assess the impact of these forces on its own position, the company must understand the structure of its competitive environment.

Exhibit 4-1. Three product life-cycle patterns.

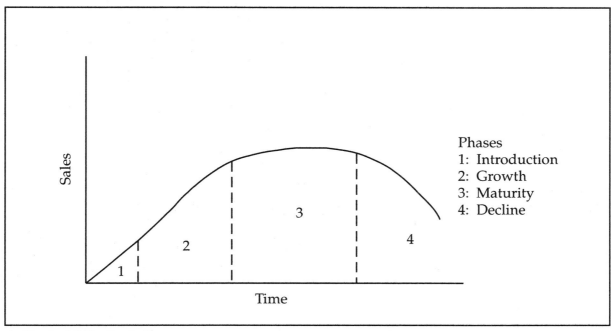

Phases
1: Introduction
2: Growth
3: Maturity
4: Decline

A: Typical Life-Cycle Pattern

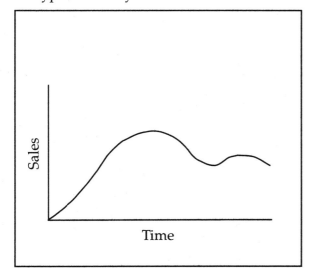

B: Cycle-Recycle Pattern

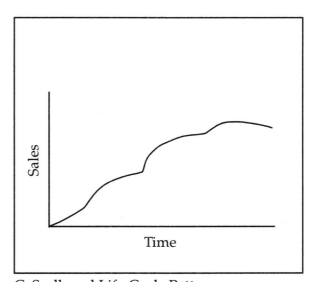

C: Scalloped Life-Cycle Pattern

This understanding must correlate the potential for market entry and exit as well as competitor behavior and reaction to the company's market actions.

The company can gauge market entry and exit from several perspectives by answering the following questions:

- How easy is it for new companies to enter the market as providers of comparable products and services?
- What barriers are there to market entry? How significant are they?
- How difficult is it for companies to leave the market? What are the implications?
- What barriers are there to exit? How significant are they?
- How readily could others enter the market through alliance or acquisition, specifically, by taking or reinforcing the position of existing competitors?

Exhibit 4-2 lists representative barriers to market entry and exit. Market developments must be analyzed within the context defined by the competitive structure. In other words, the company must analyze market developments and determine (1) if

Exhibit 4–2. Barriers to market entry and exit.

Barriers to Market Entry

1. Economies of scale or minimum operating size do no support the required investment.
2. Capital requirements for minimum facilities, equipment, and R&D exceed the financial resources of potential competitors.
3. Major transition costs would be incurred by customers changing suppliers.
4. There is restricted access to distribution channels or the services of established sources of supply.
5. Cost or production advantages, such as proprietary production technology, access to or control of raw materials, location, operational subsidies, or production efficiencies, are not available to new entrants.
6. Government regulation or public policy prohibits entry or limits competition.

Barriers to Market Exit

1. Providers have invested in specialized assets that have a low liquidation value or limited alternative use.
2. Significant fixed or sustained closure costs would be incurred, including the dissolution of existing customer or supplier agreements.
3. The products or services have strategic dependencies with other products or services sold by the company.
4. Management or owners have an emotional attachment to a product or operating unit of the company.
5. Regulatory constraints exist or could be enforced to prevent discontinuation of production or sale of the operating unit.

the opportunities created by increasing demand are sufficient to overcome the cost or difficulties of entering the market, thereby creating the potential for entry by additional companies; and (2) if the costs of market exit are so high, or disposal costs of assets so low, that companies will remain, thereby creating a more competitive situation in the market.

The company must determine if its competitive environment is hostile or passive. Specifically, it must understand the form and magnitude of direct and indirect competition from other companies. The answer comes from knowledge of competitors' market strategies as well as from the company's own strategy. If the company is in a directly competitive situation, any action it takes in the marketplace is likely to be countered by competitors. Therefore, the company must address the following questions regarding competitor behavior:

- How do competitors react to specific market developments?
- Are they leaders or followers? Are they aggressive or conservative?
- How does the company itself react to market developments?
- How may market developments change the strategic position among competitors?

An analysis of competitor behavior is important in determining the market share or level of sales that the company can expect, but it is also important in determining the price that the company can charge. In an open market, the availability of relatively comparable products inevitably results in downward pressure on prices or increased demand for product support. These pressures may result in a change in the demand function for a given product, causing it to become more price-sensitive with purchasers. In this case, the company should lessen its reliance on historical price/volume relationships, specifically when developing sales and revenue projections.

In summary, there are several market forces that influence the demand for the company's products and its market position. They influence the size and purchasing behavior of current and potential customers as well as the actions of current and potential competitors. The company must evaluate the strengths and weaknesses of its market strategy in the light of these forces. This analysis should result in identification of areas in which company strategy must be modified.

Analysis of Technological Developments

Technological developments affect the company's performance and market position in several ways. First, technological developments affect the market utility and relevance of the company's products, thereby directly influencing the pattern of sales growth. For example, if technological advancements support the development or introduction of a product that is perceived by the market to be superior to the company's products, the remaining life cycle of the company's products will be drastically shortened. This situation occurs frequently in computer and other high-technology industries. Similarly, technological advances can extend the life cycle of a product if they result in the development and introduction of features that supplement or possibly enhance the capabilities of the product. These advances may also provide benefit to new customer segments.

Second, technological developments can affect the productivity and efficiency of the production process. This will influence the cost of production and production capacity of the company. If the company is able or willing to invest in the benefits of a technological development, it may reduce its production costs or increase its product quality or quantity. This may provide the company with enhanced margins or increased demand at lower prices. However, if the company is unable or unwilling to take advantage of technological developments, it may be placed in a relatively disadvantageous position with regard to production costs. The company is likely to face downward price pressures with declining margins, or it may be forced to make additional investments in marketing and sales efforts to de-emphasize price. The impact of technology on production costs can be seen in production methods, product design, and overhead operations.

Third, technological developments can affect the productivity and cost of sales and distribution systems. An example is the impact of telecommunications on an organization and its sales force. Computers linked through telecommunications have greatly expanded the ability to maintain customer information and to make focused, cost-effective direct marketing contacts. An illustration is the rapid increase in targeted direct market selling. As a consequence, distribution middleman and associated costs are essentially eliminated. The company should evaluate the effectiveness and structure of its sales force to determine if technology can result in more cost-effective methods of sales and distribution.

Finally, technological developments can significantly affect the mix of personnel skills needed by the company. If the company plans to employ technologically advanced equipment and procedures, it must determine the skills needed to achieve the most cost-effective return on these resources. Many companies are unable to capitalize on advances in technology because they fail to understand staff skill requirements. Technological advancement, even when modest in its rate of change, can render staff skills obsolete and create the need for new and different skills. Because the process of developing skills can be time-consuming and expensive, the company must anticipate the short- and long-term impact of technology changes on the skills required in critical management, customer, research, and production functions.

In summary, technological trends and developments can have a significant impact on the competitive position of the company. Technology can quickly influence how a company maintains, improves, or loses market position relative to its competitors.

Analysis of Economic Developments

Most companies monitor economic developments, particularly those that have a significant effect on sales, interest rates, and the general cost of doing business. There are several ways in which economic developments affect the performance of the company.

First, when employment and income levels are growing, consumers tend to purchase and invest more freely. Purchases of nonessential items and services increase, and buyers become less price-sensitive. The opposite relationship obtains when poor economic conditions prevail. For this reason, the company must evaluate trends in sales within the context of existing economic conditions. It should also develop sales projections within the context of the economic conditions forecast.

Second, economic developments as they relate to financial markets and the cost of capital have numerous implications for the company's financial strategy. Cash flow is an important issue for nearly every company. As the cost of funds increases, so does the relative importance of effective cash flow management. This means that the company must not only control its purchases but also effectively manage its collection and payment policies. Most companies try to balance their credit and payment policies to support and maintain critical customer and supplier relationships.

The cost of funds also affects a company's investment strategy. The status of capital and funds markets influences the company's sense of urgency about investing excess funds and acquiring funds to cover shortfalls. As the cost of funds increases, each alternative use of funds must be evaluated against standards for expected payoff, both in return on capital and in internal investment in skills and technology. Further, it is typically difficult to acquire funds from outside sources in situations where the cash generated from operations is marginally adequate to satisfy lending or investment requirements. In these circumstances, lenders and creditors may have a growing interest in and influence on management's strategic direction.

Economic developments can also affect the perceived adequacy of the company's financial performance. For example, rising interest rates can create new uses for funds that may be more lucrative than investing in the company's operations. The payoff expected from a company, including the mix of financial return and risk, can change in a relatively short period of time, resulting in pressure to modify the standards for the company's financial performance.

The Impact of Major Social and Political Change

In addition to the three primary components of an external analysis, there are broader social trends that may affect the company. These trends must be evaluated on the basis of their implications for new opportunities and threats. In this regard, it is useful to reflect briefly on history. There was a time when events unfolded more slowly, even somewhat more predictably, than they do today. The future and its effects on business was more often a matter for speculation than survival. In a rapidly changing world, however, effective forecasting is essential to business success. It is apparent that the simpler times have gone forever.

Several recent international events exemplify the rapid rate of change in today's world. First, the dramatic changes in the political and economic structures of the countries of Eastern Europe and the Soviet Union unfolded within only a few years yet will have long-term, and perhaps permanent, effects on both business and consumers. Second, the Iraqi invasion of Kuwait precipitated a major world crisis that continues to influence the equilibrium of energy costs and trading relationships throughout the world. The economic unification of Europe and the polarization of the U.S. and Japanese economies have ongoing implications for nearly every business.

Not only is the rate of change increasing; the sheer magnitude of change is almost overwhelming. Change is the effect of innovation, which goes through a predictable diffusion cycle. For any innovation, there will be people who adopt the new technology, fashion, attitude, or behavior as soon as it is introduced. Following them are the early adopters, who become comfortable in perceiving and adopting change shortly after it is introduced. In the center are the majority, who wait for the risk of innovation to be minimized and who seek assurance that the innovation is viable. Finally, the late adopters will always include people who adopt the change simply because the pre-innovation alternative is no longer available in the market.

The diffusion cycle is as close as we can come to a rule of social and economic dynamics for successful innovation. Business planners must bring a sense of timing to their consideration of changes in the external environment. When does the anticipated development become a threat? When does it appear to be an opportunity? At what rate of speed is the opportunity or threat approaching the company or receding from it? The answer to these questions can be considered relative to the status of the change or innovation in the diffusion cycle. Is this development early in its adoption cycle? Is it peaking? Is the development fading, perhaps clearing the way for a new set of developments? Sometimes the answers to these questions must be conjectural, particularly when it is still early in the diffusion cycle. In other cases, the answers are to be gleaned from more conventional business indices such as changing revenues, market share, or customer attitudes and preferences. At times, the answers may be found in the business and popular press or in conversation with one's peers.

The balance of this section describes trends that have important business implications. The trends described are relatively new. In some cases, the validity of these trends may be questionable. Nonetheless, business planners are encouraged to weigh these thoughts against their personal experience and opinions.

For the 1990s and beyond, any company needs to consider the core of its business and that of its customers. When the company's customers are other businesses, management must determine if these businesses are part of the economic future or part of the economic past. The implications for one's own business are apparent. If all your customers are part of a mature industry, this fact may be contrary to your long-term viability and profitability.

A few examples should clarify the importance of this consideration. Nearly 85 percent of the people who will be working in the year 2000 are in the work force today. Service businesses that are highly labor-intensive are already faced with labor shortages. These labor shortages are not just quantitative; they are also qualitative. Most of the limited growth in the labor pool will consist of young people with limited literacy skills and work maturity. These labor pool entrants may also have limited English-language skills. All businesses aware of these developments need to plan for increased costs or technology investment requirements. If they do not, they will face an unanticipated labor crisis.

Another work force trend that warrants attention is seen in the real estate industry. John Naisbitt in *Megatrends* argues that high tech will never replace "high touch," meaning that people will always seek to congregate and share physical space. Specifically, he argues that the trend toward individuals working at home by benefit of computer, fax, phone, and delivery express will grow only so far because people like to work together to meet their socialization needs. By contrast, Alvin Toffler in *The Third Wave* and Dennis Kravetz in *The Human Resources Revolution* argue that the American response (or lack of response) to the child care issue combined with the level of automotive congestion will contribute to a substantial increase in people working at home. These people will be drawn together for company meetings or perhaps on a weekly basis to satisfy formal and informal needs for group cohesion and management. If Toffler and Kravetz are right about this trend, then how many new office buildings will need to be developed? And how should some portions of the existing commercial real estate inventory be disposed of? Opportunities as well as threats are presented by this scenario, because facilities suitable for periodic meetings may replace more traditional company and office facilities.

Ken Dychtwald and Joe Flower in *Age Wave* describe the aging of the American population and forecast the types of products that will be in demand as the result of this demographic trend. They identify the need for automobiles that are easier to enter, telephones with larger numbers, and architectural designs that minimize the use of stairs.

Having suggested the implication of future external developments for the company's planning efforts, we now turn to some major developments, or, to use Naisbitt's term, "megatrends," that warrant business consideration. The ten megatrends are highlighted, and the ideas of other authors noted.

Naisbitt's Ten Megatrends

1. *From an industrial society to an information society.* America and Europe are entering a historic period fundamentally comparable to the Industrial Revolution. However, instead of moving from agricultural to industrial economies, they are moving from industrial- to information-based economies. This trend is at the heart of the changes that should be monitored and considered in long-range business planning.

2. *From forced technology to high-tech/high-touch technology.* Regardless of its inherent and far-reaching potential, technology will be mastered by humans, and the human response will prevail. Humans have needs that can only be met by socializing, and, Naisbett argues, these needs will temper high-technology development. Business plans relating to research, product development, and marketing will have to factor in this high-touch aspect so that new product technology is designed and delivered appropriately.

3. *From a national economy to a world economy.* This trend is developing rapidly and has far-reaching implications for many businesses. It implies a need to reassess the importance of foreign competitors and customers as well as international ownership of production. The dramatic political reorganization of Eastern Europe and the Soviet

Union is an example of economic imperatives driving political change. If one's business has benefited from protectionist legislation or defense spending, planning must weigh the immediate impact of these influences and develop strategies for diversification.

4. *From short term to long term.* The speed of change requires more careful consideration of the focus of each business. Short-term thinking that emphasizes an immediate financial return is simply inappropriate in a changing, or relatively unstable, environment. If your environment permits you to focus only on the efficiency of the production function, you may miss the influence of environmental forces on the viability of your business. Unfortunately, many businesses face complex and dynamic circumstances in which the most efficient management of the production function has relatively low priority in planning and improvement efforts. Businesses that fail to make the transition to longer-term planning horizons will suffer most as the pace of change continues to accelerate.

5. *From centralization to decentralization.* State and local governments are becoming the most significant entities to consider if your business is anticipating legislative and regulatory impacts. A host of federal laws and regulations also remain that can affect the economics of business. However, it will be especially important to monitor the activities of city hall and state government.

6. *From institutional help to self-help.* There is a growing tendency, particularly in the United States, to do things ourselves. This trend represents a rekindling of the old ideal of self-reliance. The planning implications for service businesses may prove to be profound, moving companies from do-it-all approaches to supportive approaches. In a related matter, although the traditional nuclear family will continue to be an important consumption unit, other household arrangements are unfolding. Redefinition of the family and other self-help social structures must be considered, and not only by businesses that directly serve the aging population.

7. *From representative to participative democracy.* There is a close correlation between this trend and the increasingly important role played by state and local governments in affecting business. The continuing decline of labor unions in America and the events in Europe might be viewed as evidence that this is a worldwide phenomenon. Individualism is on the rise. Employees want to be heard and to participate in decision making.

8. *From hierarchies to networking.* Egalitarian trends in human relations and a general disaffection with bureaucracies are leading to experimentation with alternative forms of organization and administration. As a result, there is a current emphasis on more horizontal communication and a downgrading of the traditional institutional roles and channels characteristic of hierarchical organizations. The movement to matrix forms of organization relating employees to teams and functions is an example of this trend. Employee productivity and job satisfaction will be the driving forces behind these changes.

9. *From north to south.* The census indicates that the north-to-south shift in the

United States is really a shift from traditional metropolitan concentrations to somewhat smaller peripheral areas. Although many of these communities are found in the west, southwest, and southeast, considerable development can also be noted in the suburbs surrounding major older cities. Work-at-home options have led to an increasing number of people remaining in or returning to smaller communities.

10. *From either/or to multiple options.* Standardization and conformity are fading with the proliferation of life-style and consumer alternatives. This proliferation has clear implications for market planning. Market segmentation is considerably more complicated than it was in the past.

In fact, Michael J. Weiss, in *The Club of America*, provides a portrait of the nation's forty neighborhood types (or market segments) along with a synopsis of their values, life-styles, and purchasing behaviors. His book is based on a creative method of target marketing developed by the Claritias Corporation. This system permits identification of life-style characteristics through use of the U.S. Zip Code system. For companies that are providing products and services directly to the consumer, the planning implications require formidable increases in analytic precision and detail.

Although Naisbitt's ten megatrends attempt to identify major future developments, they do not address economic health, an important element that any planning process must deal with. Hugh B. Stewart, in his book *Recollecting the Future*, focuses on techniques for projecting technological, business, and economic growth. Several of his major concepts are instructive for the business planner. Rather than focusing on the boom and bust business cycle, Stewart discusses the ingredients of the long business cycle, relating the long economic wave to energy consumption data. Stewart poses this question: "Would you invest your company's money predominantly in research or in manufacturing equipment when sales are outstripping the production capabilities?" Specifically, his research shows that during strong business growth, the most cost-effective use of financial resources is further investment in the production enterprises already showing a handsome return. He further shows that the climate most conducive to innovation is after growth has been exhausted and industry finds itself in the economic doldrums with its traditional product lines. This perspective is valuable for small as well as large companies because it supports a more systematic approach to "riding" the business cycle and promoting a shift in emphasis from production to research and development when sales decline. The business plan can and should forecast economic conditions, and the relative emphasis placed on production or, alternatively, research and development and product diversification should be a well-defined contingency, predicated on the economic forecast.

Exhibit 4-3 presents a checklist of questions that can be useful in determining how prepared for the future your company is. The factors receiving a low rating should be addressed specifically in the business planning process.

In summarizing the business impacts of major social change, we should recall that we forecast because we cannot predict the future with certainty. The business planner's inability to achieve certainty should not preclude intelligent efforts to monitor contemporary events with an eye to predicting the future. The educated hunch is

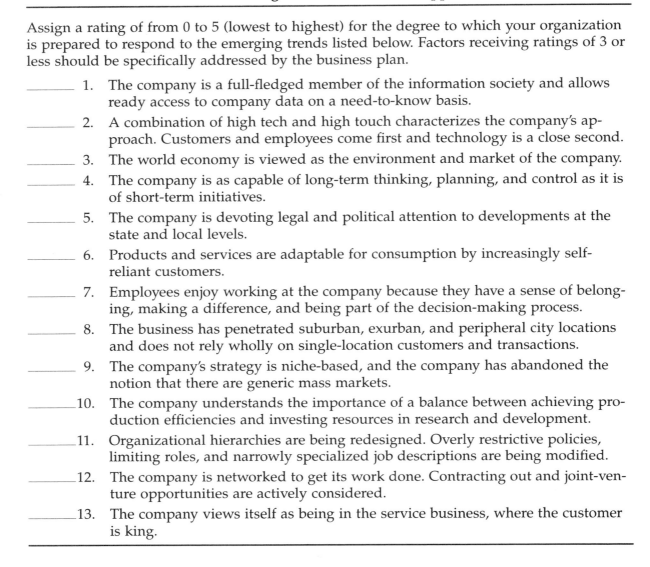

Exhibit 4-3. Megatrend readiness self-appraisal.

Assign a rating of from 0 to 5 (lowest to highest) for the degree to which your organization is prepared to respond to the emerging trends listed below. Factors receiving ratings of 3 or less should be specifically addressed by the business plan.

_____ 1. The company is a full-fledged member of the information society and allows ready access to company data on a need-to-know basis.

_____ 2. A combination of high tech and high touch characterizes the company's approach. Customers and employees come first and technology is a close second.

_____ 3. The world economy is viewed as the environment and market of the company.

_____ 4. The company is as capable of long-term thinking, planning, and control as it is of short-term initiatives.

_____ 5. The company is devoting legal and political attention to developments at the state and local levels.

_____ 6. Products and services are adaptable for consumption by increasingly self-reliant customers.

_____ 7. Employees enjoy working at the company because they have a sense of belonging, making a difference, and being part of the decision-making process.

_____ 8. The business has penetrated suburban, exurban, and peripheral city locations and does not rely wholly on single-location customers and transactions.

_____ 9. The company's strategy is niche-based, and the company has abandoned the notion that there are generic mass markets.

_____ 10. The company understands the importance of a balance between achieving production efficiencies and investing resources in research and development.

_____ 11. Organizational hierarchies are being redesigned. Overly restrictive policies, limiting roles, and narrowly specialized job descriptions are being modified.

_____ 12. The company is networked to get its work done. Contracting out and joint-venture opportunities are actively considered.

_____ 13. The company views itself as being in the service business, where the customer is king.

the pragmatic alternative to analysis paralysis and is clearly much better than doing nothing in the midst of a whirlwind of change.

Legislative and Regulatory Influences

Legislation and regulatory policies, by enforcing deregulation, competitive industry and market structures, and international or interstate trade agreements, or by offering government procurement, affect the ability of companies to generate revenues. These actions also affect their ability to control wage and benefits costs, labor relations, occupational safety and health standards, environmental quality, infrastructure assessments, and other forms of taxation. Government policies, in short, permeate every facet of a company's operations and influence market, technological, and economic developments.

Using the Results of an External Assessment

At the beginning of this chapter, we stated that the purpose of an external analysis was to identify threats and opportunities that have implications for the future performance of the company. But how does a company determine if an external development constitutes a threat or an opportunity, and how can it understand its ultimate significance? Asking the following key questions may help:

- What is the impact of external developments on the company's strengths and weaknesses?
- Do some of its strengths become weaknesses? Do some weaknesses become irrelevant in the projected situations?
- What is the impact of external developments on the company's operating and financial strategies?
- How easily can strategies be modified either to take advantage of favorable trends or to respond to unfavorable developments?

The answers to these questions provide the basis for an assessment of the company's strengths and weaknesses that focuses on the future rather than on the past. The company naturally regards its production facilities and distribution system as significant strengths. But what if technological developments make these "strengths" less cost-effective than alternatives? Similarly, growth in key customer segments may not represent a real opportunity for the company unless it can adapt its market strategy to gaining a share of that new demand.

The identification of threats and opportunities will not be very useful to the company unless it can determine the significance and possible effects of these forces. Thus, the company must evaluate the relationship of the various threats and opportunities to each aspect of its business strategy. A format for identifying threats and opportunities and assessing their impact on the business strategy is presented in Exhibit 4-4. The major issues identified in this analysis must be addressed in developing a business strategy and plan that is truly responsive, not merely reactive, to developments in the external environment.

Managing Adaptation to Change

Understanding the company's critical relationships is an important first step in managing these relationships. However, the strengths and weaknesses of each organization

Exhibit 4-4. Analysis of external developments.

Type of Development	Impact On					Opportunities Created	Threats Represented
	Marketing	Production	R&D	Org. & Mgmt.	Finance		
1. Market developments							
A. Composition of and growth in customer segments							
B. Product growth and life cycle							
C. Competitor actions							
2. Technological developments							
3. Economic developments							
A. Overall employment and income							
B. Availability and cost of funds							
4. Legislative/ regulatory developments							

are different. The ultimate benefit of understanding these external relationships is to integrate this information in ongoing as well as strategic decisions. Raymond E. Miles and Charles C. Snow, in *Organizational Strategy, Structure, and Processes,* describe the concept of a "learning organization." This concept is based on the critical ability to effectively collect and integrate external information. The learning organization is one that can adapt dynamically to trends in external developments. By implementing an adaptive cycle and organizational structure, it can make ongoing operating adjustments to external and strategic developments. Further, the adaptive cycle focuses on decentralized information collection and action, which results in strategic objectives being integrated in all levels of organizational decision making.

The Miles and Snow model views organizational adaptation as a continuing response to three broad problems:

- The entrepreneurial problem—selecting viable markets and objectives
- The engineering problem—creating a technology and process to serve the selected markets
- The administrative problem—developing an organizational structure and managerial processes to coordinate and control the selected technology and to ensure the innovative activities needed to maintain the company's viability.

External information must be incorporated into these elements of the company's strategic direction. Adaptive behavior enables the company to use this information to refine its understanding of its position in the environment and to make integrated modifications in these three primary elements of its strategy. Perhaps the greatest strategic challenge in any company is to overcome the built-in forces that resist internal change. These forces may include:

- Top management's tendency to defend a system or course of action that it has developed
- Reward systems that stifle innovation
- Reliance on a static set of external information sources
- Emphasis on strategic initiatives to the exclusion of current deficiencies
- A focus on problems rather than solutions

For this reason, the process of learning and adaptation must involve a broad range of perspectives and individuals within the organization. Getting all personnel to buy into the strategic direction and adaptive cycle of the company can be as important as the content of the strategy. A philosophy and practice of controlled experimentation can supplement the collection of external information and enhance the capacity for learning within the company. This process implies nontraditional, decentralized forms of management and organization as well as a willingness to acknowledge and respond to weaknesses.

Implementing Learning Organization Concepts

This chapter has broadly covered a number of philosophical concepts and considerations. The baseline external analysis is an important first step in determining which of the learning organization concepts are appropriate for your organization. The company's business and strategic plan should use the external analysis to identify specific concepts that will be implemented to meet the company's needs. Within the context of creating a deliberately focused organization, a number of broad-based techniques can be implemented.

Techniques for Collecting Relevant External Information

The overall objective of collecting external information is to have broad involvement in the activities, organizations, and institutions that comprise the company's external environment. Here are five techniques for increasing company awareness and involvement:

1. *Make members of the management group responsible for tracking and reporting on relevant external developments.* This is an apparent but often overlooked technique. Members of top management should be rewarded for their effectiveness in cultivating sources of industry and related information. They should also be responsible for developing a communication system within their spheres of management control to bring together all information obtained by employees. Active participation in industry organizations and development of peer group relationships can extend the company's network. Involvement in and commitment to external activities by top management provides an essential source of information.

2. *Use an external board of directors to "coopt" external information.* The use of an external board can link the company to technological, economic, legal, and political trends and institutions. The company should be careful to select board members who are truly independent and unrestrained by any commitment to special-interest groups. Privately owned organizations can also take advantage of external board benefits through specific charter provisions ranging from advisory discussions to active independent oversight. Unfortunately, complications surrounding the legal liability of corporate board members must be carefully considered in order to attract the best talent and broadest perspectives.

3. *Use outside consultants on a selective basis.* Outside consultants can be a valuable source of information regarding developments in an industry. However, few consultants possess the broad range of insight and skills necessary to the strategy of the company. The use of several consultants to obtain this broad input should be carefully planned, because uncoordinated and inconsistent recommendations by a number of consultants can result in conflicting initiatives.

4. *Hire for strategic positions with the aim of obtaining valuable sources of external infor-*

mation and perspective. A balance between promotion from within and external hiring can perpetuate strengths while bringing new ideas and information sources to the organization. Hiring criteria should reflect the informational or institutional weaknesses and objectives of the company. Key positions in management as well as operational or technical functions can be identified for this purpose.

5. *Encourage and reward external involvement by all employees.* The collection of external information should not be a management function exclusively. The strategic involvement of employees in specific organizations can be part of the goal setting and objectives for individual performance. This form of involvement by employees in technical and social organizations can provide useful sources of information.

Techniques for Integrating External Information

The information obtained from the external environment is useful only if it can be integrated by top management into the strategic direction of the company, and by managers into ongoing operational decisions. The objective of integrating this information is to give the company the opportunity to anticipate the need for change and to adapt to it in a timely and responsive manner. The following steps will help:

1. *Implement departmental and organizational structures that facilitate communication.* Team-based organizational structures offer an opportunity for integrating information that may not be found in traditional forms of organization. Teams can be formed on a project or functional basis so that team decisions and actions will reflect input from a variety of information sources. Also, interdepartmental task forces can effectively tackle problems that may be less easily addressed within individual departments. Team forms of organization may have the additional advantage of improving employee morale and developing personal commitment to the company.

2. *Organize work teams that are market-linked.* Work teams that are directed to specific market or product functions can focus their attention and efforts on opportunities. This market orientation also limits the confusion that can be created when teams are too broadly focused. A market-matrix form of this type requires a decentralization of decision making and a broad range of decision-making authority within a clearly defined scope of responsibilities.

3. *Make management responsible for team development, communication, and coaching.* Management's responsibility should be to foster the functioning of work groups. Management should also be the link between work groups so that work group involvement and communication are coordinated. Further, management should guide and coach work group activities so that decisions are consistent with the company's overall strategic objectives. The emphasis in management's coaching of work groups should be on how decisions are made—the process of decision making.

4. *Develop a decentralized process for formal planning and budgeting.* A bottom-up planning and budgeting process should be based on overall company objectives.

Within these objectives, work groups and divisional management teams should use their creativity to integrate their sources of industry, technical, economic, and competitor information in product initiatives.

5. *Cultivate effective methods for communicating the company's strategic objectives and values.* Informal gatherings, employee recognition, and newsletters can all be used to convey management's objectives and values relative to its competitors and outside influences. This knowledge can more effectively be integrated with employees' understanding of their role in the company, the company's position relative to external influences, and the framework that this information provides for routine daily management and operational decisions.

6. *Reinforce effective information collection and integration behavior through reward, promotion, and recognition.* An adaptive orientation by employees should be considered in the company's criteria for reward and promotion. Effective behavior among teams and individuals should be recognized and broadly communicated throughout the organization.

7. *Develop cross-functional skills and perspectives through interdepartmental employee transfers, nontraditional career paths, and interdisciplinary teams.* A blend of perspectives can result in creative interpretation of existing information. As a result, decisions made within one functional area of the company can be made in the light of issues or implications that may affect other functional areas.

Techniques for Creating a Learning Orientation

The nature of the company's industry will determine the extent to which adapting to the external environment is critical to success. For some, acting quickly will be more important than having completely accurate information. In any case, the truly effective company must foster a management system that effectively experiments and bases future decisions on the knowledge obtained from experimentation and adaptation. The following steps are conducive to the appropriate learning environment:

1. *Develop a systems analysis orientation among work groups.* Work groups need analytic skills and methods to understand the processes they perform. This knowledge is critical to understanding the causes of existing problems as well as the potential influence of external forces. The focus on cause and effect should be a consistent method underlying all forms of innovation.

2. *Invest in employee and work group training that contributes to effective experimentation and adaptation.* Communication, analytic, and work group skills are important to the technical, managerial, and production work force. Investment in training is a powerful indication of a company's commitment to a progressive and adaptive approach.

3. *Adopt a research/action/analysis approach to innovation.* While the research and action components may be apparent, many companies do not adequately analyze the reasons for innovations succeeding or failing. As a result, the opportunity for learning

from innovation is limited. Also, a fear of failure may develop if only the results of successful innovations are communicated.

4. *Encourage employee participation in innovation and adaptation.* Firsthand experience can be the greatest force in bringing reluctant or cautious employees into a learning and innovation process.

5. *Monitor the extent and longevity of innovation and adaptation.* Too often, things are assumed to be fixed until broken. An attitude favorable to continuous improvement is needed for the company to adapt to changes in its environment.

6. *Create situations in which controlled innovation and experimentation will not adversely affect the core business of the company.* Subsidiaries and joint ventures may be vehicles for experimental or prototype projects.

7. *Make external analysis, integration, and learning a priority of top management.* The analysis, training, reinforcement, change in management processes, and innovation described in this chapter do not come without cost. Management must actively direct resources to areas of change and innovation that will improve the functionality of the company, even though they may not provide immediate financial return.

To conclude this chapter, we must re-emphasize the importance of external analysis, integration, and adaptation as fundamental processes of the company. If effectively implemented, an adaptive orientation and related skills can provide a means of risk management for the company. Small to mid-size organizations may look upon formal efforts of this type as excessive or unnecessary. However, effective external analysis and integration do not require an in-house planning department or volumes of data. They require an understanding of the company's own strengths and weaknesses as well as of its competitive and operating environment. They also require a willingness to implement basic structural techniques to ensure adaptation to external developments. Finally, they require an investment of time and energy, though this need not be an intimidating or overly complex process. The risks and long-term implications of simply reacting to the external environment are far too great.

Chapter 5
Strategy and Goal Setting

The assessment of the company's internal and external environments establishes an informational framework that allows it to make informed decisions about its future. Setting goals and strategies initiates the process of translating the results of the environmental assessment into meaningful business decisions and plans. Through the environmental assessment, the company has profiled its recent history on each key dimension of performance, including factors related to marketing, production, R& D, organization and management, and finance. The company has also made some assessments about areas of operation that require changes or improvements in response to identified weaknesses and threats; further, it has targeted additional areas in which changes or improvements can be made to take competitive advantage of the strengths and opportunities.

Setting goals essentially reverses this diagnostic process, turning it into a decision-making process regarding future directions and actions. These directions and actions focus on the same key dimensions of performance that were analyzed earlier.

Goal setting, as we explain in this chapter, involves three interrelated concepts: goals, objectives, and strategies. Because these concepts are easily and often confused, we provide a brief definition of each concept and describe the qualities that should characterize practical goals and objectives for the company. In the balance of the chapter, we focus on the process of translating the results of the environmental assessment into specific goals, objectives, and strategies.

Defining Goals, Objectives, and Strategies

A goal is a statement of desired direction or achievement, the end to which efforts are directed. Typically, a goal relates to establishing or improving something. Areas for improvement are identified through the environmental assessment. They are those areas about which the organization can say, "Here is what it is, but this is what we want it to be." GAP analysis, that is, the difference between what is and what ought to be, is a useful approach to setting goals. Thus, goals should come directly from the results of the environmental assessment.

Goals should be distinguished from objectives and strategies, terms that will be used extensively in this chapter. We define a goal as a general statement of desired direction or improvement. It may or may not have a specific time frame attached to its achievement. An objective is a *measurable* statement or accomplishment. It has a specific measurable outcome, a time frame for its accomplishment, and possibly a specific commitment of resources or budget. A strategy is a method of achieving either goals or objectives or both. Strategy is the art of devising or employing plans toward the realization of a goal. From this definition, it should be clear that goals must precede strategy. Exhibit 5-1 illustrates the distinctions among these concepts.

Well-formulated goals and objectives have the following characteristics:

- They are suitable in the sense that they are supportive of and consistent with a company's basic purposes and values. If the company has a mission statement, each goal clearly supports this statement.
- They provide a basis of measurement and are measurable over time.
- They are feasible and attainable in the context of the company's industry, market, and internal capabilities.
- They are supported and accepted by the people in the organization who are responsible for achieving them. In other words, people perceive them as attainable and compatible with the basic values of the company.
- They are flexible enough to accommodate unforeseen circumstances but firm enough to provide and ensure proper direction.
- They are written and communicated in such a way that they can be easily understood by all personnel who are responsible for achieving them.
- They are linked in a comprehensive framework so that all goals and objectives are basically consistent with each other and supportive of the company's basic purposes.

Goals and objectives with these characteristics tend to provide a clear, consistent sense of direction for the company and its work force.

The following checklist should be periodically consulted during the goal and strategy development cycle:

Checklist for Goal Evaluation

☐ Is the goal consistent with the company's mission statement or stated direction?
☐ Will clearly definable outcomes result from achievement of the goals?
☐ Is there a definable time frame for determining if the goal has been reached?
☐ Is the goal realistic? Can it be reasonably attained by the people responsible, and with the resources they will have available?
☐ Have the resources needed to achieve the goal been obtained, or are there definite plans to obtain them?
☐ Are the goals compatible with each another?

Exhibit 5-1. Examples illustrating distinctions between goals, objectives, and strategies.

Goal	Objective	Strategy
1. Win the war.	1. Retake France.	1. Invade Normandy.
2. Increase revenues by 25% within 5 years.	2. Increase annual sales to 50 million units in 5 years with a maximum increase in marketing expenses of 10%. Increase company's market share by 15% in 5 years.	2. Decide on subobjectives for the following areas: • Sales organization and productivity • Promotion, advertising programs • Product pricing • New market penetration • Distribution system, i.e., uses of various distribution channels and costs • Geographic and customer segment sales • Product/service mix
3. Regain market share.	3. Increase sales units to X; change cost per unit to Y.	3. • Improve quality. • Aim advertising at competition. • Improve product line.

☐ Are any of the goals in conflict with existing policies, practices, or procedures?

☐ Will achieving these goals provide a satisfactory position for the company? In terms of profit? market share? production? quality?

☐ Are the goals acceptable to the people responsible for achieving them?

☐ Does the company have access to the capital (cash or other) that will be required?

A strategy is simply the set of decisions that defines the overall approach to achieving the goals and objectives. Strategies will ultimately be broken down into specific tactics and action plans, but, as suggested in preceding chapters, strategies should be developed for the basic components of the company's operation—that is, for marketing, production, R&D, organization and management, and finance.

In summary, goals, objectives, and strategies are very important concepts in the planning process. They define the types of decisions that should be made throughout the process. The primary concern for the company is to recognize that effective planning requires decisions as to priorities and directions for improving performance, levels of performance to be achieved, and actions to achieve the desired performance levels. In addition, these decisions must be consistent with each other to provide useful guidance. The error made by many companies is not establishing a clear and direct linkage among these levels of planning decisions. This produces a fragmented, unclear sense of direction that may inhibit rather than facilitate effective performance by the company.

Establishing Goals

There are two primary questions that must be asked and answered with regard to establishing goals and objectives. First, what information will the company use to set its goals and objectives? Second, what process will the company use to analyze this information and make its decisions? Alternative approaches are available to answer each question.

Goal setting must be based on an analysis of information regarding the current situation of the company. Companies typically use one of two basic approaches in analyzing information in order to set goals and objectives. The first is a proactive approach, which analyzes historical performance trends and external developments, then develops goals on the basis of a future outlook that reflects the trends and patterns identified. The second is a reactive approach, which identifies available resources and develops goals on the basis of alternative, desirable uses of these resources. In both approaches, a point is eventually reached where the goals must represent a reconciliation between the resources available or obtainable and an analysis of the environmental conditions expected.

Companies that perform effectively over the long term use the proactive approach. Therefore, the process described in this chapter and throughout the book reflects this approach. The proactive approach is more open-minded; that is, it considers the full range of options and is market-oriented. It provides a stronger basis for identifying and considering all potential opportunities and significant threats to the company.

Most presentations on effective goal setting suggest that there should be extensive participation by the personnel who will be involved in achieving the goals. This participation tends to promote understanding and commitment and, consequently, motivation to attain the goals. However, there are situations in which goals are most appropriately established directly by top management. This is true when top management possesses all of the knowledge and information required to make quality decisions; when top management requires or desires a significant redirection; or when the company is in an environment in which there is a significant degree of risk associated with the various goal or strategy alternatives. Even when goals are directly set by top management, however, they will be more readily accepted by other personnel when the goals are supported by an objective and complete analysis of the company's current and anticipated position.

In What Areas Should Goals Be Established?

Goals provide the basis for developing the major business strategies of the company. Consequently, goals should relate to marketing, production, R&D, organization and management, and finance. In addition, the company may want to establish some overall goals for growth, profitability, or return on investment that cut across functional boundaries. In the process of developing goals and measurable objectives, the company is not only defining basic directions and courses of improvement in its operations; it is also defining standards and reflecting assumptions about the future that will be used to build the operating plans for each major business strategy (see Chapters 7 through 10). With these considerations in mind, we now turn to goal setting in each strategic area.

Setting Market Goals and Strategy

In most business situations, the primary purpose of market goals is to maximize overall sales and revenues. A secondary purpose is to achieve maximum productivity from sales, promotion, and distribution activities. The development of a coherent strategy requires that goals, and subsequently objectives, be established for (1) sales of specific products and services; (2) sales to specific customer segments; (3) sales by geographic area, and (4) sales by channel of distribution.

These four goals are obviously highly interrelated. In developing the goals, the company should employ a matrix approach to ensure that they are consistent and feasible in terms of the structural realities of the marketplace. A matrix approach simply correlates goals or performance objectives in two different business or operational dimensions. For example, sales goals for specific products and services can be correlated with sales goals for specific customer segments. Through matrix analysis, the company is able to determine if the sales goals for specific products and services and those for specific customer segments reflect the anticipated needs and purchasing behavior of these customer segments. The matrix approach thus allows the company to decide if goals that made sense at an aggregate or total level still make sense at a disaggregate level. A series of matrices that can be used to set market goals with internal structural consistency is presented in Exhibit 5-2, parts A, B, and C. Each change should be reviewed as to its realism. For instance, it makes no sense to set a goal for a customer that is greater than that customer's total need for a product.

The development of these goals should occur in conjunction with the development of policies and operating assumptions for each element of the marketing strategy. These policies and assumptions relate to pricing; the organization, level, and productivity of the sales effort; the level, composition, and productivity of promotion and advertising efforts; and the structure and productivity of the distribution system. These factors obviously have a direct impact on the level of sales that can be achieved. Conversely, the desire to achieve a specific level of sales dictates, to a certain degree, the prices that can be charged, the level of promotion effort required, and the like.

Exhibit 5-2. Customer goal-setting matrices.

A. Customer Goal-Setting Matrix for Products/Services

Product/Service Group	*Customer Segment*							*Total Sales in Units*
	Name of customer[b]							
Product/service[a]	Sales (in units)[c]							

[a]Enter specific product/service in this column.
[b]Enter names of specific customers in this row.
[c]Enter number of units of sales in this row.

(continued)

Exhibit 5-2. (*continued*)

B. Customer Goal-Setting Matrix by Geographic Areas

Geographic Area	Customer Segment							Total Sales in Dollars
	Name of customer[a]							
Area 1								
Area 2								
Area 3								
Area 4								
Area 5								
Area 6								
Area 7								
Area 8								
Area 9								
Area 10								

[a]Enter specific customers in this row.

Thus, the development of goals, policies, and operating assumptions is an interactive process that may require several iterations to achieve the necessary congruence.

What information should the company use to establish operating assumptions and to develop sales goals and strategic policies? The internal assessment generated historical information on precisely these same relationships between sales levels and strategic variables—for example, between prices and the productivity of marketing efforts. The external assessment provided a context for interpreting historical relationships and trends, particularly in terms of the probability of their continuing in the future. The company should initially develop an objective analysis that essentially represents an extrapolation of the historical trend line into the future and then adjust it to reflect the anticipated impact of relevant market developments and other external

C. Distribution Channel Goal-Setting Matrix for Products/Services

Product/Service Group	Distribution Channel							Total Sales in Units
Product/service[a]								

[a]Enter specific product/service in this column.

forces. However, this analysis is only a starting point because it represents what is likely to happen if the company pursues the same policies and strategy it has in the past.

At this point, the company must engage in the interactive process of exploring the feasibility of various strategic policies and operating assumptions and their impact on sales levels. This process is more art than science and is highly dependent on the industry and the market knowledge of the company's managers and advisers. Therefore, it becomes critical that knowledgeable people—including outside advisers when appropriate—be involved in this process. It is equally important that the process be objective and grounded in a realistic assessment of probabilities that are based on market facts, not on a set of hopes and dreams.

The analytical process used to establish appropriate market goals and strategies should produce decisions in five areas:

1. Sales organization, size, and overall productivity standards
2. Prices to be charged for the product/service and, if appropriate, a schedule of price changes for the period covered by the plan
3. Sales goals by product/service group, customer segment, and geographic area
4. Major objectives and expenditure levels for advertising and promotion efforts
5. Organization, overall productivity standards, and costs of the distribution system

With these decisions, the company has the structure to compute revenue levels, which are a function of prices and unit sales, and marketing and sales expenses, which are a function of the costs associated with sales, promotion, and distribution activities.

In concluding our discussion of market goals and strategy, it is worthwhile to reemphasize a point we made earlier. The sales goals and market strategy drive the development of the goals and strategies in other areas—for example, production and finance. Therefore, the practicality of the overall business plan is determined to a large degree by the reality and feasibility of the sales goals and the market strategy operating assumptions.

Setting Production Goals and Strategy

Historically, the primary purpose of production goals and strategy has been to minimize production/service costs and, in the process, to maximize the contribution margins of the company's products and services. However, in today's environment, this purpose must be achieved within a strict context of quality standards designed to support the company's market strategy—that is, to maintain or expand the demand for company products and services.

Among the issues that must be evaluated in order to set quality goals are the following:

- Do we know our present quality position?
- What quality do our customers expect?
- What quality does our competition provide?
- What are the economics of quality?

Very clearly, if the company is not already utilizing a total quality management concept, then one goal should be to evaluate TQM for its applicability to the company's situation.

The development of a coherent production strategy requires that goals, and subsequently objectives, be established for production capacity, both overall and for specific products/services; for labor productivity; for equipment productivity; for production overhead costs; and for production cost standards for specific products and services. Like marketing, these goals are highly interrelated.

More important, these goals are based on operating assumptions and policies regarding several factors. These factors include:

- Direct labor costs, including wages and fringe benefits
- Investment in new plant and equipment
- Cost of raw materials and supplied products/services
- Methods and cost of transportation to distribution channels
- Level of supervision
- Required overhead support
- Achievement of desired levels of quality

The operating assumptions and policies established in these areas reflect the degree to which the company is able and willing to control production costs. For example, a company's position relative to the organization of its labor force and suppliers affects its ability to control workers' wages, fringe benefits, and the cost of raw materials. Similarly, the company's willingness to change its sources of supply and distribution, which may be based on long-standing relationships, affects its ability to control costs in these areas.

Again, what information is available to help the company establish operating assumptions and policies? The internal assessment provides data to support an objective analysis of labor costs, labor productivity, levels of supervision and their apparent effect on productivity, equipment and facilities cost and utilization, and costs of supplied materials and services. Further, the external assessment identifies opportunities for increasing productivity or reducing costs through technological enhancements and identifies the potential impact of economic developments on supplier relationships and costs. Thus, information is available to develop an objective, adjusted trend analysis of production factor costs if the historical strategy of the company remains intact.

There are several areas in which a company can and should consider adjustments to its basic strategy. Potential adjustments include:

- Expanding or revising production/service capacity, which must obviously be considered in the light of the sales goals
- Increasing or changing the locations of production/service facilities to obtain access to a better labor pool or reduce transportation costs, which must also be considered in the light of the customer segment and geographic sales goals
- Investing in new equipment to increase productivity or quality levels
- Restructuring relations between the factors of production—that is, labor and equipment—to increase productivity or reduce costs
- Subcontracting all or part of the production process to other companies or importing components if shorts or long-term cost savings can be realized and quality standards maintained

The cost of making the adjustment must obviously be weighed against the expected payoff in terms of reduced costs or increased revenues.

Further, the assumptions regarding production factor costs are affected by the assumptions and goals that are established in other strategy areas. We have already discussed the interaction between market and production strategies. Any substantial change in the product/service sales mix within the market strategy can have a significant impact on the production strategy. For example, retooling may be required or new skills and supplier relationships may be needed. The production strategy is also affected by R&D goals, particularly those related to new product development and introduction, and by organization and management goals, particularly those related to compensation and management and supervision ratios. Thus, the process of developing operating assumptions and policies for the production strategy should recognize identified weaknesses and probably improvements in related strategy areas.

The analytical process used in establishing appropriate production goals and strategies should produce decisions in the following areas:

- Standard costs for supplied materials, products, and services that are inputs to the production process
- Productivity standards for all significant production/service activities or processes
- Standard unit costs for each product/service
- Supervisor-to-staff ratios for each worker group
- An estimate of fixed operating costs
- Production capacity by product group, both overall and within individual facilities
- Production overhead structure

The decisions regarding sales levels provide the structure for computing total production costs, evaluating the feasibility and reasonableness of sales goals, and developing estimates of operating profitability. We will discuss the process of translating these goals and policies into a detailed production plan in Chapter 9.

Setting Research and Development Goals and Strategy

The evaluation of the R&D strategy should be based in large part on the degree to which the company has been able to keep pace with and be responsive to external developments. The need for specific R&D goals and a formal strategy must be determined by the results of the internal and external assessments. The R&D goals, and ultimately objectives, relate to the development, improvement, and refinement of products/services and of the production process. The focus of product development is revenue generation; the focus of process development is cost reduction or improved productivity.

The company must first decide whether the R&D goals are necessary and appropriate. If not, the process obviously stops. However, this decision should not be easily reached. By their very nature, R&D activities and goals relate to long-range developments. The need for R&D activities and goals should be based on a futuristic look at the company's industry and operating environment. This is as true for service and distribution companies as it is for manufacturing and construction companies. When the market is becoming increasingly competitive and customer preferences and buying behavior are becoming increasingly price-sensitive, then R&D goals are critical. If the company can compete on factors other than price, it is in a stronger position to increase contribution margins and profitability. If the company must compete on the basis of price, it needs to plan and make investments in its operations that will improve productivity and cut costs.

Once a company determines that the R&D goals are required, it must determine its ability to pursue those goals. Capability can be evaluated in terms of staff skills, facilities, and financial resources to support the R&D effort. When the company has the financial resources but lacks all or part of the staff skills and facilities required, it must choose between two options:

1. If product or process development is a fairly immediate or one-time need, a company can contract with another organization to obtain the required capabilities. In fact, relying on outside R&D may be a developed long-term strategy. Such vehicles as university grants may enable research to be conducted without incurring an in-house facility cost.
2. If product or process development is a continuing or long-range need, a company can set as one of its goals the acquisition and development of the skills and facilities.

On the other hand, when a company lacks the financial resources, it may have to reevaluate the extent of its need for R&D goals. If the need is verified, the company should give the goals priority and develop ways of acquiring or generating adequate financial resources.

R&D activities represent costs, often significant and sometimes intangible, to the company. If R&D goals are set, a management and operating plan for achieving them should be developed. Because the structure and content of the R&D operating plan are so variable and so dependent on the goals, we will discuss the development of this plan in Chapter 8.

Setting Organization and Management Goals and Strategy

The primary purpose of organization and management goals and strategy is to provide the skilled work force with an organizational structure appropriate to achieving its goals in marketing, production, R&D, and finance. Productivity standards have been explicitly developed as part of the market and production strategies. Of course, these must be consistent with the overall productivity standards that are reflected in the organization and management strategy. The development of a coherent strategy requires that goals, and subsequently objectives, be established for the following:

- Productivity in all worker categories, but particularly in sales, production, clerical/administrative support, and management
- Mix of skills and composition of the company's work force
- Supervisor-to-worker ratios, span-of-management control, and the like
- Development of staff skills
- EEO/affirmative action
- Compensation and fringe benefits programs
- Expansion or reduction of the work force

There is a high degree of relatedness among these goals, as is true of other strategies. But more than in marketing, production, or R&D, the development of organization and management goals is highly dependent on the values and orientations of a company's management. These will affect choices relating to:

- Internal versus external development of staff skills, that is, the extent to which a company hires and trains inexperienced people rather than skilled, experienced personnel
- Company approaches to motivating staff performance
- Financial and nonfinancial rewards for performance
- Informal versus formal management control systems

These values define how the company treats its people, and this is the critical issue to be addressed through the organization and management strategy.

The company should have fairly precise information on worker productivity. The primary organization and management goal should relate to improvements in worker productivity. In fact, the focal point for every component of the organization and management strategy—for example, the assignment of authority and responsibilities, screening and selection of personnel, performance tracking and reporting systems, training of personnel, compensation levels, and so forth—is improved productivity both of individual staffs and the company as a whole. In setting goals, the company should use its productivity data and the results of the environmental assessment (see Chapters 3 and 4) to identify specific areas in which human resource management policies and procedures, organizational structure, staff skills, and administrative and management procedures need to be revised or developed in order to improve productivity.

The analytical process used to establish organization and management goals and strategies should produce decisions on the following:

- Productivity standards for the various worker categories
- Compensation and fringe benefit programs for all personnel (Note: This does not mean specific salary levels for each staff person, but rather the structure within which managers will set salary levels.)
- An organizational structure that reflects assignments of authority and responsibilities
- A performance management system structure, including measures of performance, reporting procedures, and so forth
- Skills development or training objectives for the company
- Staff expansion and skills acquisition objectives for the company
- Objectives for improvements in the company's management and administrative procedures, for example, communications, planning, and decision making

Decisions on these matters obviously have some impact on the marketing and production goals, particularly those for worker productivity levels and compensation policies. Thus, there must be a reconciliation between the organization and management goals (and their expected impact on productivity) and the operating assumptions used to develop the marketing, production, and R&D goals. A format for developing organization and management goals from the results of the environmental assessment is presented in Exhibit 5-3. We discuss the translation of these goals into an operational plan for organization and management in Chapter 7.

Setting Financial Goals and Strategy

Financial goals and strategy have two main purposes. First, they should support the capability of a company to generate profits through its operations, that is, through sales and production. Second, they should effectively manage the funds generated through operations and ensure the continued financial solvency and growth of the company. An effective financial strategy can supplement the company's operating profits, but the primary purpose of the financial strategy should be to ensure that the company has the financial resources required to support its ability to generate operating profits.

The basic structure for setting financial goals and strategy was defined by the components of the internal assessment. The financial strategy must simultaneously

Exhibit 5-3. Organization and management goal-setting form.

Factor	Results From Environmental Assessment	Improvement Objectives and Actions
1. Understanding of company's goals and objectives		
2. Understanding of company's organizational structure		
3. Effectiveness of management and work procedures		
4. Effectiveness of organizational communication procedures		
5. Effectiveness of organizational climate		
6. Effectiveness of personnel management policies		

address the issues of liquidity and short-term solvency, asset management, debt management, overall profitability, and cash flow management. In setting goals for each of these components of the financial strategy, a company must consider the impact of leverage on its potential profitability. Briefly, leverage defines the impact on earnings, or before-tax profits, of changes in sales levels.

There are two types of leverage. Operational leverage is determined by the extent to which the company's cost structure, excluding financing or interest expenses, is comprised of fixed versus variable costs. The higher the percentage of fixed costs, the higher the operating leverage will be and the stronger the impact of changes in sales levels on earnings or profits will be. For example, for a given rate of sales decline, the rate of decrease in earnings will be higher as the degree of operating leverage increases. Similarly, for a given rate of sales increase, the rate of increase in earnings will be higher as the degree of operating leverage increases.

Financial leverage is determined by the extent to which the company has incurred fixed financial obligations, that is, interest payments. The same basic relationship exists as with operating leverage except that the impact is on return on equity or earnings per investor share. In general, the higher the percentage of debt as a component of the level of investment, the stronger the impact of changes in sales levels on earnings per share will be. Leverage is an important consideration in a financial strategy because, depending on the degree of confidence in sales projections, earnings can be improved by increasing or decreasing the degree of leverage.

As an example of the decision process regarding operating leverage, let's look at the alternatives associated with certain items. If it is believed that sales volume will be highly volatile, then perhaps the appropriate decision is to leave certain assets variable over the short term. Conversely, a stable sales volume enables longer-term (usually with lower cost) asset decisions. The following table illustrates some of the financial alternatives available.

Asset	Options for Short-Term Flexibility	Options for Long-Term Stability
Building space	Rent, short-term lease, sublet	Build your own facility, enter a long-term lease
Transportation fleets	Rent, short-term lease	Buy, long-term lease
Labor	Use of part-time personnel or subcontractors	Hire and develop your own personnel
Cash	Credit line, factoring of receivables or inventory	Issue stocks or bonds

The starting point for establishing financial goals, however, is to review the company's financial position. From this analysis, the company should identify the need to increase liquidity, the opportunity or need to improve asset utilization or possibly to invest in additional assets, the opportunity or need to increase or restrict the use of debt to finance operations, the need to increase profit margins on sales, and the need to improve collections to maintain adequate cash flow. The company should then set target levels for each of the ratio indicators.

In addition to targets for these indicators, a company needs to establish standards or policies regarding:

- A minimum return on investments in new equipment and facilities
- The use of operating and financial leverage
- A collection period, interest charges to customers, and price and payment discounts

These policies and standards obviously have an impact on the goals and strategies in each of the strategy areas previously described. It is important that the goals and strategies in each area be reconciled in order to provide a consistent framework for preparing the operational and financial plans.

The ratio targets and the supplemental standards, when correlated with the sales and production objectives, provide a sound structure for preparing company's budgets and financial statements, which we discuss in Chapter 10.

How Should Goals and Strategies Be Used?

The goals, policies, standards, and operating assumptions—that is, the outcomes of the process described in this chapter—define the structure within which the detailed operating and financial plans can be developed. This course has not, as yet, produced words, numbers, or tables that are likely to be included in the business plan document. However, we have laid the foundations for developing these products in a meaningful and valid way. The strength of a business plan lies in the validity of the goals and strategies that are developed through the process outlined here.

The goals and strategies provide a critical link between the results of the environmental assessment and the specific objectives and implicit action strategies in the operating and financial plans. The direction and assumptions reflect management's perceptions and expectations regarding the future. At this point in the planning process, it is important to recognize the degree of uncertainty, and therefore of risk, that is associated with the assumptions and consequently with the goals. The company must set goals that represent its most intelligent assessment of the future, but if other possible assessments exist, the company should develop backup assumptions and strategies that provide a basis for effective contingency planning.

PART
TWO

Chapter 6
Preparing for Plan Assembly

The development of a strategy and identification of operating goals described in Chapter 5 is the last step prior to actual preparation of the business plan. The next critical step is to translate the strategy and goals into a plan that will help direct the ongoing operations of the company.

The strategy and goal-setting process is typically driven by upper management. However, the more detailed planning efforts at the functional level of the company should involve all of management as well as some nonmanagement-level personnel. For example, the strategy and goals related to finance may be developed by an upper-management team including the chief financial officer and the controller. Department planning activities for the financial plan may include these officers as well as one or more financial analysts, the head of the credit function, and others involved in various aspects of finance and accounting. These second-tier managers, although they may not have the broad company or industry exposure to effectively contribute to the strategic planning or goal-setting activities, are essential participants in the detailed company and departmental planning efforts.

The completed strategy and goals for the company should be summarized at a level of detail that will allow functional managers to develop and refine detailed plans. Ideally, this information should be distributed as part of a planning package so that the information available to all employees participating in the process is consistent.

The requirements for developing the organization, sales, production, and financial plans are generally similar. Each of these plans requires creativity. Department managers should be challenged to find new ways to realize the goals and strategy of the company. Most important, they must be encouraged to work together to identify and evaluate alternatives that cross departmental boundaries.

In most circumstances, the optimal plan for achieving specific company goals requires compromise among various departments. For example, minimizing the carrying cost of inventory and finished goods may require a trade-off that entails manufacturing products in lot sizes that increase the per-unit costs. In these situations, the overall goals of the company must take precedence over the goals of individual departments.

Several rules of thumb should govern the transition between the more conceptual strategic planning phase and the more detailed operational planning phase:

• *Demonstrate by example that top management places a high priority on the operational planning process and is committed to its completion.*

• *Introduce the detailed planning process in a way that clearly defines the level of effort expected from each functional area of the company and specifies the involvement required of each individual.* If this is not done, the initial iterations of plans will be inconsistent and incomplete. The planning process should include time for detailed analysis at the departmental level, interdepartmental working sessions to resolve differences and integrate assumptions and information, and one or more group sessions in which departmental representatives work together to refine plans and analyze contingencies.

• *Prepare an information package that describes the detailed operating plan process and specifies meetings, deadlines, and information requirements.* Managers may develop their own work plans for analyzing information within their departments.

• *Avoid performing detailed department planning as a piggyback on the budgeting process.* Most budgeting processes tend to be exercises in making incremental department-based adjustments to operations. In contrast, department-based planning efforts should challenge department managers to rethink their programs and operations to meet the goals and strategic direction set for the company. A budgeting process may be appropriate, after the completion of the planning process, to develop the level of detail needed to control the actual expenditures for program activities.

• *Develop a data and information requirements list to ensure that there is adequate guidance and structure to the analytic efforts of departments.* This list should describe the specific information to be considered but should not constrain creativity.

• *Begin the department-level planning activities with a kickoff session in which expectations and time frames are identified.* Upper management should review in significant detail the refined strategy and goals established for the company and each department. Questions should be solicited to ensure a thorough understanding.

• *Identify individuals who can facilitate group sessions, particularly among departments.* These individuals should not have a direct interest in the plans of any one department and should not represent upper management. The objective is to facilitate discussion in order to resolve differences and integrate plans to accomplish the strategic direction and goals. Departmental cooperation is essential to the success of this process.

• *Make attendance at interactive sessions mandatory and see that it is considered a high priority.* Recognize the contribution of outstanding individuals.

• *Standardize the form in which information is to be prepared by the departments.* For example, a set of microcomputer spreadsheets can be used to identify the information required and to present it in a format that can facilitate its consolidation for analysis.

This can make analytic sessions more productive by focusing them on the impact of specific changes on operations or assumptions.

• *Include representatives of total quality management or similar employee work groups in departmental planning.* These representatives can provide input on the topics, issues, and alternatives being addressed by work groups.

• *Provide examples to guide each department in translating goals into action plans, alternatives, and programs.* Plans should be described as the group of activities necessary to accomplish an identified goal. Alternatives should be described as various forms of plans, and programs as the combined efforts of several plans.

• *Incorporate participation in planning efforts into the individual performance goals for participants.* Participation in planning activities can be an effective means of motivation, recognition, and professional development.

• *Emphasize upper management's intention of maintaining an ongoing planning process after the initial business plan is completed.* The initial exercise may be difficult, and commitment to a high-quality effort can be reinforced by the intent to make continuous improvements in the process.

• *As part of upper management, oversee the completion of department milestones and plans within the specific time frames.* However, department managers, cooperating with each other, should be responsible for actually developing department plans.

In summary, the detailed planning process should be organized and managed in ways similar to any other large project. Parameters and guidelines must be developed, roles defined, and deadlines identified, and someone must oversee the completion of the process and the quality of background work that is done. What makes the business planning process unique is the requirement for interaction between departments and functions, which may be unprecedented in the company. Thus, the process may require a significant change in culture and behavior. This aspect of business planning presents the greatest need for leadership and direction.

Chapter 7
Developing an Organization and Management Plan

The overall purpose of the organization and management plan is to define a structure for the company that will allow it to meet its business objectives in the most effective manner. This method must address four overall objectives. First, it should define the basic management structure of the company, including the assignment of managerial and administrative authority, responsibility, and accountability. Second, it should identify objectives and actions for improving the company's management and administrative systems. Third, it should identify objectives and actions for fulfilling the company's work force requirements, including skills development. Finally, the plan should address the financial resources required for its execution.

Developing an Appropriate Management Structure

An appropriate management structure is critical to the success of the company. The structure should be described in an organizational chart that reflects a general division of responsibilities among staff positions, specific assignments of responsibility, authority, and accountability among management and supervisory positions, and an identification of the skills required for each critical position. The type of management structure that is most appropriate will vary according to the company and industry.

Type of Business

The nature and scope of the company's operations have a significant effect on the organizational structure. For example, if the company has highly interrelated products or services that lend themselves to common use of marketing, sales, and production capabilities, then a functional form may be most effective. The functional form centralizes the administrative activities of the company to achieve administrative economies.

It also centralizes administrative control. If the products or services are not highly interrelated and there is substantial volume in each product/service group, then a product/service divisional form may be more effective. A divisional form decentralizes product line management, typically including production planning, controls, distribution, and management accounting. Higher-level division plans and operating results may be managed by a central administrative structure that coordinates among product or divisional groups.

Type of Performance Measures

The organizational structure should influence the type of performance measures that are used. In a functional approach to organization, performance measures should relate to the factors and outcomes that each functional manager can control. For example, the marketing and sales manager can have a significant, direct effect on sales and revenues, and his or her performance should be measured on that basis. However, the marketing and sales manager may not have full control over profitability, which will be strongly affected by production costs and pricing. In this case, it is most appropriate to measure the performance of the marketing and sales manager on factors such as sales and revenues, marketing and sales expenses, and marketing and sales productivity. Divisional managers may have a much broader scope of responsibility and authority, including administrative management. Their performance measures should reflect the range of responsibilities associated with this broader scope of authority.

Key Management Personalities

The appropriate management structure should be consistent with the styles and personalities of key management personnel within the company. The success of many companies is strongly influenced by the strength of key personnel in critical positions. The management structure should support and supplement the strengths of these individuals. However, the company should be careful to distinguish between supporting individual strengths and covering for weaknesses. The performance of key personnel should be evaluated relative to their capability to meet specific skill requirements. Significant organizational changes that simply buttress the weaknesses of individuals may prove to be dysfunctional.

Nature of Competition

The management structure should support the company's method of competition within its industry. In today's competitive and rapidly changing business environment, the most effective structure is one that is adaptive to change. Companies involved in rapidly changing industries may seek more decentralized and adaptive organizational structures. Those involved in lower-margin products may require the efficiency that centralization can provide.

Customer Orientation

The relationship to the company's customers should also influence the structure. For example, a customer service or value-added method of competition will require decentralization of authority to make timely customer decisions. This form of decentralization can best be accomplished within the framework of clearly defined customer service and company strategies and policies that can be consistently implemented with discretion by personnel with direct responsibility for client service.

Company Competitive Strategy

The specific intent behind any organizational restructuring program should be carefully considered. Any significant restructuring effort implies a change in strategy or method of competition. The corresponding redesign of the company's organization will have significant implications for production, service, and management capacity. Many companies have found that downsizing programs intended to improve competitiveness have improved efficiency at the expense of effectiveness. As a result, they have been unable to capitalize on upswings in demand.

If these considerations are properly considered and integrated with other organizational strategies and decisions, the management structure will support the company's management needs rather than create additional ones.

The Form of the Structure

The form of management structure strongly influences the composition of positions represented in the company, particularly at supervisory and management levels. Consider the implications of the functional structure illustrated in Exhibit 7-1A. In this functional arrangement, the company needs a well-defined mix of technical specialist skills. Because the company's operations require that these skills be brought together in a cohesive manner, the individuals in these positions must cooperate or the company must provide specific management direction and oversight to ensure cooperation.

The divisional structure illustrated in Exhibit 7-1B shows a different set of requirements. In this situation, it is necessary to have strong generalist skills at the management level. Managers must be capable of integrating the various functional and general management activities that occur within the division. This structure also requires that management have relevant product/service and industry-specific knowledge.

Exhibit 7-1. Three types of organizational structure.

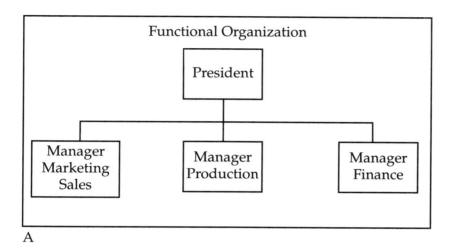

A

B

Exhibit 7-1. (*continued*)

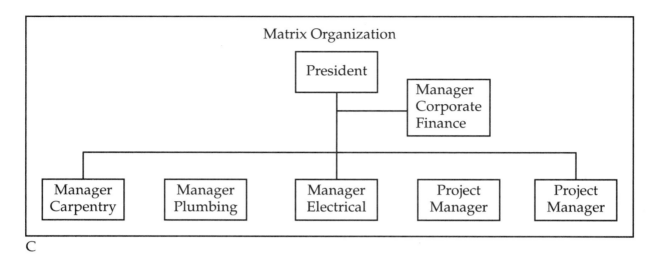

C

The matrix management structure illustrated in Exhibit 7-1C provides a blend of technical specialization and general management skills. The matrix structure is generally most appropriate for companies that work on a project basis, where each project requires a mix of diverse technical skills. This form of organization has the benefit of distinguishing between technical management and administrative management. The separation of responsibilities allows technical managers to focus on project outcomes rather than on administrative management details. It also results in administrative management consistency across technical project boundaries and a focus on integration and coordination.

The appropriate management structure will evolve as the company grows. As it expands its operations, it may need to move from one form to another. The company must periodically evaluate its current situation, its plans for the future, and its management needs. It should also contemplate the implied shifts in management authority inherent in the acquisition of new product lines, management reorganization, replacement of key personnel, regrouping of responsibilities, entrance into new markets, and planning for new production facilities or technologies. This often means that one of the company's greatest challenges is to develop effective, adaptive managers.

The analogy of building blocks can be applied to plans for organizational change. In a growth environment, the company should build the functions of the organization that will support its growth and strategic objectives. This building should precede growth, not follow it. For example, a strategic move into new products and inventories may require specialized industry skills among product managers. Acquiring or developing these skills early in the implementation process will provide a building block for a smoother and more efficient transition into its new markets. Restructuring in anticipation of changing product management responsibilities may increase the effectiveness after the transition.

Organization and management structures can change over time. However, acquiring and developing the management skills necessary for leadership, growth, and profitability is a more difficult and demanding task.

Implementing the Structure

The organizational structure may initially be selected by the company but eventually becomes a function and vehicle of the company's strategy. It provides the blueprint for assignments of authority and responsibility. In order for the structure to be effective, the company must be able to communicate in detail the scope of responsibilities for each management, supervisory, and professional position. The formal description of position responsibilities may include the following categories of information:

- Overall function or role of the position within the company's structure
- Specific responsibilities of the position
- Authority delegated to the position to make decisions, supervise or direct staff, expend funds, and access information
- Critical outcomes and success factors that define the effectiveness of activities performed within the position's scope of authority and control
- Measures of performance or the basis on which performance will be evaluated, ideally consistent with critical outcomes and success factors
- Accountability and reporting relationships with superiors

These categories of information are similar to but somewhat different in focus from those included in a traditional job description. Rather than specifying all tasks to be performed, a position description emphasizes the four components of effective delegation—responsibility, authority, outcomes, and accountability.

The organizational structure and position descriptions should also define the skill requirements for each unique position. The company should define these requirements in terms of fairly specific skills and capabilities rather than just general education and prior work experience. This approach provides a more effective framework for evaluating, selecting, and developing personnel to meet specific organizational requirements. Further, a comprehensive skills profile can provide evidence that the company has thoroughly considered its personnel requirements and has developed an objective means for evaluating the capabilities of key personnel. This may be important in communicating confidence to investors and customers.

An appropriate management structure is the key mechanism for turning the company's plans into action. Many well-formulated plans fail in implementation because of an inappropriate structure or poorly defined position requirements. In fact, as almost anyone with a reasonable amount of experience in the work force knows, an ineffective management structure can have a dysfunctional impact on all aspects of the company's performance and competitive position. The cost in time, money, and lost opportunity of replacing someone in an incorrectly specified position can be devastating.

Today's rapidly changing business environment requires an adaptive and responsive work force. A culture of learning and adaptation can be reinforced by ongoing attention to customer service, efficiency, and improvement. Overly rigid job specifications and procedures can sometimes constrain adaptation. Conscious efforts are often needed to communicate the reasons for strategic shifts in responsibilities and job functions.

An environment that provides constant learning is a philosophical goal that will provide long-term competitive benefits to the company and its work force. This goal is implemented through worker involvement, effective communication of each worker's role in the strategic direction and success of plans, and ongoing investment in training and retraining. This goal must be reinforced through the recognition and rewards system so that individual goals become aligned with and supportive of the company's goals. Individual growth and career development opportunities must exist in order to maintain a stimulating environment that will attract and retain top-performing personnel.

Developing Effective Management and Administrative Systems

An effective management structure and personnel capability is one part of the organization and management puzzle. The company must also develop and implement effective systems to support that structure. The specific nature of these systems varies, depending on the company and its management style. However, most companies set up systems for planning, purchasing and inventory control, financial and operational information, production management, quality measurement, personnel/human resource administration, compensation management, and customer relations. Typically, a system includes a defined functional scope of activity, relationships to other systems, methods of collecting and analyzing data, and controls to ensure consistent outcomes.

The company must periodically assess the strengths and weaknesses of its management and administrative systems. The assessment must incorporate planned changes in the company's management structure to achieve management systems that are mutually supportive. Several questions should be asked when evaluating management systems:

- *Does the system provide value directly to the customer or contribute to the effectiveness of the company's activities?* Does the system provide information required for regulatory compliance? If not, there may be compelling reasons to discontinue or change the system.
- *Is the expense and organizational effort of supporting the system justified by the value of its output?* If not, restructuring to achieve greater efficiency may be justified.
- *Could restructuring or introducing new technology to the system provide competitive advantages?* Internal systems, such as quality programs, can be competitive if the value they provide is perceived by customers as differentiating the company's product or service from those of its competitors.

- *Can the required information or control be obtained as a function or by-product of another system?* If so, consolidation of procedures, information, or reporting could improve efficiency.
- *Does the system generate output in a form that supports decision making and management at the appropriate level of the organization?* Systems designed to support one form of organization can become obsolete when the organization changes or new technology provides new system capabilities.
- *Is the system consistent with and complementary to the company's strategy and method of competition?* Management controls and systems should be designed to answer questions about the extent of the company's success in accomplishing its strategic objectives.

Goals for improving management and administrative systems were established in step 3 of the planning process discussed in Chapter 5. These goals should be translated into a specific action plan that describes the company's efforts to develop or refine these systems. Responsibility for the plan should also be assigned and estimated costs and budgets given. Exhibit 7-2 is a format for planning within each of the major systems of management control.

Developing an Effective Work Force

The company must identify the type and mix of the personnel skills it needs to satisfy the requirements of its plans. An analysis of required skills must address existing needs as well as the needs created by new markets, products, strategies, or technology. Any management structure or systems changes are likely to require new skills or behaviors.

There are two basic approaches the company can take to developing its work force. It can recruit and hire people with critical skills or it can hire less experienced people and develop these skills through training programs. Each approach involves significant costs and potential risks. When the company hires experienced people, it usually pays a premium in the form of higher compensation. There is also some risk that skills developed elsewhere will not be transferable to the company and its environment. When the company hires less experienced people, it obviously incurs costs for training, but it also assumes some risk regarding the learning capacity of new employees. Alternatively, the company can train existing staff to meet new or unfilled skills requirements.

Skills deficiencies should be identified and compiled within the functional or divisional structure of the company. The source of this information must be the performance appraisals of individual staff members and the requirements for implementation of new or refined systems and procedures. The appraisal of staff performance is typically the result of formal performance evaluation systems or the observations and perceptions of managers and supervisors. The less formal method of observation and perception often lacks the requisite objectivity and consistency. However, the more

Exhibit 7-2. Format for a management and administration systems action plan.

Action Step	Monthly Timetable												Responsible Staff	Estimated Cost
	1	2	3	4	5	6	7	8	9	10	11	12		
Inventory control														
Financial information														
Production tracking and measurement														
Marketing and sales information														
Billing, collections, and payments														
Personnel/human resources management														
Compensation management														

Exhibit 7-3. Format for a staff development/acquisition plan.

Skills Deficiency/Need	Number of Staff/Positions Involved	Approach	Time Frame	Estimated Cost
Management				
Supervision				
Professional				
Production				
Support				

structured systems may not measure the performance characteristics critical to the success of the company unless these characteristics are routinely grounded in the company's evolving strategy.

The company should develop a complete profile of skills and development needs that is based on formal and informal sources of performance information. For each unfilled need, the company must assess its magnitude and decide on an approach to meeting it. Each approach should be defined in terms of informal on-the-job training, in-house training that may require external trainers, formal outside training programs, transfer of staff within the company or acquisition of staff skills from outside the

Exhibit 7-4. Format for a management and administrative budget.

Cost Item	Quarter				Total for Year
	1	2	3	4	
Salaries and fringe benefits					
Executive					
Support					
Facilities					
Space					
Utilities					
Equipment and supplies					
Equipment rental					
Supplies					
Systems development and improvement					
Staff development and improvement					
Total					

company. Each of these approaches involves tangible costs that should be estimated. A planning format for staff development needs, strategies, and related costs is presented in Exhibit 7-3.

Developing an Estimate of Management and Administrative Expenses

In order to begin the process of estimating management and administrative expenses, the company should break down expenses into fixed, variable, and special, one-time components. The fixed component typically includes executive and support staff compensation, facilities costs, office supplies and equipment rental, telephones, and utilities. Variable costs typically include temporary staff, professional services, and a minimum amount of training based on staff size. Special costs generally relate to the costs of the systems and staff development improvement objectives that have been established.

The company may or may not have relevant historical and planning information to begin developing an accurate estimate of management and administrative expenses. In either case, the company should prepare a buildup of expenses based on system flows. Personnel requirements, space, communication, and related expenses should be attributed to specific administrative functions or systems. As systems are developed or modified, their support requirements can be translated into expense additions or reductions. The composite skill and resource requirements will reflect the overall organizational and administrative program of the company.

Expenses should be estimated for the whole year and for each quarter. If the company uses the time-phased approach for planning the activities identified in Exhibits 7-2 and 7-3, it can obtain a reasonable estimate for each quarter in which it will incur the related costs. Exhibit 7-4 is a format for estimating management and administrative expenses.

Chapter 8
Developing a Sales Plan

In previous chapters we described the planning process—specifically, developing goals and strategies for marketing, production, R&D, organization and management, and finance. These goals and strategies outline the framework from which detailed operating plans can be developed.

This chapter focuses on the development of a sales plan. A sales plan requires refined estimates of expected sales in units, which are critical inputs for planning the company's production capacity. Anticipated unit prices for each product or service are further refined to reflect the assumptions inherent in sales and promotional programs. These refined price targets must build from the analysis of historical trends, market developments, and expected market dynamics. Market-based promotion and distribution strategies are therefore the foundation for assumptions and strategies for production, unit sales, pricing, and sales expense.

In previous chapters, goals and policies were established for overall sales by product group, customer segment, and distribution channel. General pricing goals, based in part on the historical scope and productivity of the sales and marketing program, were identified for product/service groups. Finally, objectives and expenditure levels for advertising and promotion and for the costs and productivity of distribution systems were developed. This preliminary information must now be refined into a coordinated plan that can be managed and monitored as part of the company's overall operational plan. The failure to integrate the sales tactical plans with the company's other functional plans is one of the most common and significant weaknesses of traditional businesses.

The marketing and sales plan requires:

- Translation of sales and marketing goals into tactical product management plans
- Development of market and unit tactics supported by promotion programs
- Refinement and management of the distribution system
- Modification of pricing initiatives
- Management of the marketing and advertising budget
- Communication and coordination within the company

Translating Strategic Sales Goals Into Tactical Plans

Although an estimate of annual sales has been developed through the goal-setting process, further detailed sales and marketing planning is needed. Tactical plans provide the primary means of management control for the company during the course of the year. Unless the sales objectives are translated into tactical plans, the company will be unable to manage and control the marketing and sales efforts. At a tactical level, the marketing and sales program is the primary means of influencing revenues throughout the year.

A first step is to refine sales goals into quarterly sales objectives. A quarterly breakdown serves several useful purposes. First, quarterly sales objectives provide a manageable time frame for tactical plans. The tactical status of most sales and marketing initiatives can be gauged within a three-month planning and budgeting parameter. Quarterly review of leading indicators and benchmarks can provide a basis for modifying market and sales initiatives, particularly in relation to the actual revenues being generated. Second, quarterly sales objectives are important indicators in planning and managing the cash flow position of the company. Because they affect production and financial management, the quarterly sales objectives should reflect an assessment of when sales are expected to occur during the year.

For most companies, sales are not evenly distributed throughout the year. Because sales are subject to cyclical patterns of purchasing behavior by customers, more than 25 percent of sales may occur in some quarters and less than 25 percent in others. However, if the variability is influenced by cyclical rather than trend factors, the quarterly sales distribution should remain relatively consistent over the years. The company must consider the historical distribution of quarterly sales for each product and service group. However, factors identified in the external analysis must be considered with regard to their effect on the timing of sales.

Tactical sales and marketing plans require the coordinated involvement of the managers of finance, administration, production, and personnel as well as of the managers of the sales and marketing functions. The tactical sales and marketing plan is frequently prepared in draft or proposal format and modified by the input of the company's upper functional managers. Critical assumptions, such as the availability of products to meet the anticipated sales demand, can be made only with input from production managers. In a truly market-driven company, key sales and marketing assumptions have basic implications for all upstream activities, from production to purchasing.

The most important reason for effectively integrating the sales tactical plan with the company's other functional plans is to achieve a balance among the company's business objectives. Maximizing revenues, typically the primary goal of the sales function, will in fact be dysfunctional if it requires inefficient production scheduling, excess carrying costs, excessive cash requirements, and so forth.

The initial development and ongoing management of quarterly sales results and related modification tactics will be effective only if the result is a coordinated adjustment throughout the company. In a stable environment, quarterly adjustments can be

communicated through the formal planning and management process. In a more volatile sales and technology environment, less procedural and more timely methods may
be necessary.

Developing Market Share and Unit Tactics

The life-cycle stage of each product is an important first consideration in refining sales
forecasts on a market share and unit basis. Complementary or interdependent groups
of products should be considered as distinct components of the overall product mix.
For existing products, the total potential market share may include existing or historical unit sales as well as a new or growth component of potential unit sales.

Service companies should group services in a similar manner, so that the ability
or capacity to provide a service will depend on an inventory of time, available staff,
specific skills, and equipment support.

Quarterly sales goals should be a buildup of unit projections within each of the
product groups. Quarterly goals may contain ranges of unit sales so that high, moderate, and low unit projections are presented for each group. In a relatively stable market, moderate projections should reflect historical sales patterns, adjusted for known
or booked new sales. High unit productions for each product group should be based
on the upper limit of existing or planned production and distribution capacity. The
lower unit projections for each product group should be based on the minimum production necessary to achieve basic economies of scale. Any product group projections
based on historical sales data should be modified in consideration of the following
factors:

- If new or refined products/services are introduced during the year, they may
  affect the pattern of both overall sales and the sales of product groups. This will
  be particularly true if the new products are complements to existing products.
  Similarly, if new or refined products replace existing ones, the company must
  subtract the historical effect on sales levels and patterns of the products that
  are being replaced. This will eliminate any double counting.
- External developments may have a significant impact on historically cyclical
  patterns of consumer purchasing. As an example, discounted vacation packages
  and health club memberships may influence the historical patterns for the purchase of swim wear.
- Upgraded or expanded advertising and promotion campaigns also affect purchasing behavior, at least in the short run. Quarterly sales objectives should
  reflect the timing and expected impact of planned advertising and promotion
  efforts.
- Planned price changes during the year may have a positive or negative effect
  on demand and, consequently, on the pattern of sales.

In summary, the anticipated pattern and distribution of sales should reflect both historical patterns and relationships and the impact of new or external developments.

Exhibit 8-1. Percentage of total sales by quarter.

	Percentage of Units Sold by Quarter				*Total Units Sold During Year (000s Omitted)*
	1	*2*	*3*	*4*	
1987	20	30	35	15	1,000
1988	20	25	35	20	1,250
1989	20	25	35	20	1,400
1990					
Forecast	20	30	30	20	1,750

Exhibit 8-2. Unit and dollar sales by quarter (000s omitted).

	Unit and Dollar Sales by Quarter				*Total for Year*
	1	*2*	*3*	*4*	
Units	350	525	525	350	1,750
Avg. unit prices	$ 5.00	$ 5.00	$ 5.25	$ 5.25	—
Sales	$1,750.00	$2,625.00	$2,755.00*	$1,840.00*	$8,970.00

*Rounded to nearest $5.

Exhibit 8-1 shows XYZ Corporation's historical quarterly percentage of sales for 1987 through 1990. The forecast year is estimated based on historical relationships. Exhibit 8-2 estimates total quarterly sales based on estimated unit sales for the year, percentage of sales per quarter, and average unit price.

After the quarterly distribution pattern has been established, the company can use this information and the annual sales goal to develop forecasts of the number of product or service units to be sold in each month. This "smoothing" of sales within quarters can be estimated by considering the timing and impact of initiatives in each quarter, such as promotional programs and changes in production lead times. Obviously, the goal in timing is to maximize the impact on revenues. We have discussed the interaction between prices and levels of demand, and the effect on revenues, in the internal diagnosis of the company's capabilities. The approach to this analysis reflects two points. First, sales forecasts should be developed for individual products/services, and second, sales forecasts should be based on pricing and product or service units rather than on generalized revenues.

There are two reasons for this approach to the analysis:

1. From a marketing, production, and organizational perspective, sales do not occur in dollar terms; they occur in product or service units. Effective planning of marketing, production, and organization and management activity requires a valid estimate of the number of units sold.

2. Customer demand and sales are a function of the price, utility, and availability of products. The number of units consumed is a function of need and price. Any valid forecast should, therefore, be based on an analysis of consumption patterns, market saturation, and price sensitivity. If forecasts are developed on the basis of production ranges, then the impact of any subsequent adjustments in pricing and sales on other functions of the organization can more easily be evaluated.

The unit approach or level of activity may be used even if the company provides services rather than products. This is also true for companies that supply products with accompanying or supporting services. In service companies or in the service component of a manufacturing or distribution company, planning in terms of service units establishes a basis for estimating staff and other organizational requirements.

Developing Estimates of Marketing and Sales Expenses

Marketing and sales expenses can be categorized for planning purposes as being one of three types: fixed, variable, or single-event expenses. For purposes of planning, fixed expenses are relatively stable within the time frame of the planning horizon and do not materially fluctuate with changes in unit volume. Some examples of fixed expenses are a minimal in-house sales force, basic marketing and advertising efforts, and distribution system costs. Variable expenses change in proportion to the level of unit or sales volume. Some examples of these expenses are any required expansion of the sales force, sales commissions, travel expenses, and distribution costs based on volume. Single-event expenses may include special promotion or advertising efforts or costs for establishing a new distribution channel. Single-event expenses may be recurring or nonrecurring but are nevertheless distinguished as being special initiatives. The company should use these basic categories to differentiate among types of marketing and sales expenses and to schedule these expenses over the time frame covered by the business plan.

The company should next refine the cost analyses and goals for the following areas:

- Productivity standards for sales activity
- Objectives and expenditure levels for advertising and promotion efforts
- Organization and productivity standards for the distribution system
- Unit volume for each product/service group by market or geographic service area

Once quarterly and monthly sales objectives have been identified for each product/service group, they should be refined for individual geographic areas if different distribution channels are assigned specific geographic markets. Alternatively, the domestic and international components of sales should be refined, particularly if exporting requires fundamentally different or unique sales programs or distribution approaches. Sales objectives for markets or geographic territories require consideration of numerous factors, including the historical allocation of sales, the mix within areas, the anticipated mix, and the growth of distinct customer segments.

With this information, the company should develop refined, composite quarterly estimates of marketing and sales expenses based on the buildup of the sales and marketing plans for each product/service group. The process for completing this refinement includes the following steps:

1. Fixed marketing and sales expenses should be consolidated from the plans for each product/service group. Overlaps in assumptions for staffing, space, and other fixed expenses should be eliminated.

2. Variable marketing expenses should be consolidated from the plans for each product/service group. The overall advertising, promotion, and distribution program budget should be accumulated and analyzed as a function of projected unit volume, based on the planned organization and staffing support included for each product group.

3. The reasonableness of the consolidated fixed and variable sales and marketing expenses should be assessed. Historical cost relationships and benchmark comparisons should be used. If comparable information is not available, procedures should be developed to track and analyze expense information at an appropriate level of detail for ongoing comparative and planning purposes. If expense data are maintained on the basis of market or geographic areas, then this assessment of reasonableness should be considered.

4. The accumulated expense relationships should be revised for internal and external factors anticipated during the course of the projected time frame. For example, inflation in salary and operating expenses should be incorporated if its impact will be realized. Other changes should be considered, such as sales productivity, cost standards for marketing and sales activities, and economies of scale that may be achieved through new promotional initiatives. As a result, the fixed and variable unit cost relationships may increase or decline when a specific level of activity is achieved.

5. Special or single event expenses should be scheduled according to the timing of the activities. For example, expenses should be identified at that point in the year when special advertising or promotional campaigns will be conducted and costs incurred. A separate schedule of major promotional campaigns should be accumulated along with the timing for these expenses.

From this information, quarterly and annual totals for marketing and sales should be compiled. Exhibit 8-3 shows the historical relationship between variable selling and marketing expenses to sales. Exhibit 8-4 provides estimates based on the historical relationships of quarterly selling and marketing expenses.

Other considerations when forecasting marketing and sales expenses include:

• The size of the marketing and sales activity may reach a critical mass such that higher sales levels may be achieved without proportionate increases in costs.

Exhibit 8-3. Historical sales and variable sales expenses (000s omitted).

Factor	1987	1988	1989	1990 (Forecast)
Sales	$4,900	$6,387	$7,627	$8,970
Variable sales expenses	$ 100	$ 130	$ 150	$ 180
Variable promotion expenses	50	70	85	100
Variable distribution expenses	20	25	30	53
Total variable marketing expenses	$ 170	$ 225	$ 260	$ 333
Variable marketing expense to sales ratio	3.47	3.52	3.41	3.71

Exhibit 8-4. Marketing and sales expense by quarter (000s omitted).

	Marketing and Sale Expenses by Quarter				Total for Year
	1	2	3	4	
Quarterly sales	$1,750	$2,625	$2,755	$1,840	$8,970
Variable marketing expense to sales ratio	3.71	3.70	3.70	3.70	3.71
Variable marketing expenses	$ 65	$ 98	$ 102	$ 68	$ 333
Fixed expenses	$ 30	$ 30	$ 30	$ 30	$ 120
Special events expenses	$ 20	$ 52	$ 18	$ —	$ 90
Total marketing and sales expenses	$ 115	$ 180	$ 150	$ 98	$ 543

- More efficient methods for marketing, sales, promotion, or distribution may be identified for implementation. The company may assume that the variable marketing expense relationship will apply uniformly to each quarter, without regard to the specific volume of sales in any one quarter.
- Special expenses may not necessarily be incurred in each quarter. The schedule for these expenses should reflect the nature of the marketing objectives and expended timing relative to achieving sales. To minimize the negative impact of a price increase on demand, the company may plan to initiate special promotional efforts to differentiate its product from others on a basis other than price.

Pulling Revenue and Expense Objectives Together

The quarterly and annual expense objectives should, of course, be summed across all product/service groups and market and geographic areas to obtain a total picture of planned volume, revenues, and expenses. The summary may reflect the range of high, moderate, and low sales levels or simply be the accumulation of outcomes determined by management to be the most likely.

At this point, it is useful for the company to determine the organizational implications of further economies in sales, promotion, and distribution. A further reduction in marketing and sales expense may have undesirable implications such as a reduced capacity to respond to sales volume that is greater or different in mix than forecast. However, any offsetting seasonality or certainty of unit forecasts among product groups may support further refinement of expenses.

The buildup of revenues and sales and marketing expense will reflect target pricing at this point in the analysis. Pricing refinements should be considered as one means of maximizing revenues or building strategic market share. As a whole, the forecast mix of products and services may be very achievable, but not strategic in the sense of innovation or market leadership. The diversification among the product groups may include a number of higher- and lower-margin products. It may be desirable to test the price sensitivity of the market with price increases or obtain entrance into desirable markets through pricing refinement.

The composite impact of refinements or aggressive price testing can be evaluated from an overall company perspective. A highly aggressive pricing structure will increase the likelihood of not achieving the sales and revenue forecast, so management's strategic decisions in this regard must be communicated to the sales force. Sales incentives, pricing flexibility, and price transitions may be incorporated into an aggressive pricing decision. Unique availability, functionality, reliability, or customer loyalty may support aggressive pricing. The opportunity for aggressive pricing may exist for a finite period. During this time frame, customers may obtain access to alternative products or begin a transition to other sources. Exhibit 8-5 illustrates the impact of discounts on XYZ's sales.

Price reductions or "loss leaders" may be refined when the sale of one product will support the sale of another, higher-margin product. A secondary use of strategic price reductions may be to reduce inventory, particularly of products that will be made obsolete by innovation or redesign.

The macro view of pricing and mix of products gives management an important

Exhibit 8-5. Discounted sales by quarter (000s omitted).

	Sales by Quarter				Total for Year
	1	2	3	4	
Sales	$1,750	$2,625	$2,755	$1,840	$8,970
Discount %	4	4	5	5	—
Total Discount	$ 70	$ 105	$ 137	$ 92	$ 404
Net Sales	$1,680	$2,520	$2,618	$1,748	$8,566

opportunity to strategically invest in the introduction of new products, to maximize revenues, and to minimize inventory obsolescence in the mix of products and services in the company's portfolio.

Linking With the Research and Development Plan

In preceding chapters, we stated that research and development (R&D) objectives and plans flow from the market analysis and thus are directly linked with the market strategy and the sales and revenue plan. Research and development activities include production technology as well as product development. The research and development plan is an important adjunct to the sales and marketing plan.

The research and development program should produce a current timetable for initiating and completing specific phases of the research and development process. These phases are often referred to as (1) conceptualization, (2) prototype development, (3) prototype testing, (4) refinement, (5) selective market introduction, (6) final refinement, and (7) market introduction.

The R&D process will affect the sales and revenue plan once commercial applications of R&D efforts are identified. The timing of new product development or modification and introduction will directly influence the competitive position of the company. For this reason, an effective planning link between the R&D and sales functions is a strategic necessity, particularly for firms that must compete on a features or technology basis in a highly competitive industry.

As new or refined products and services are introduced to the market on a selective pilot or a full-scale basis, several possibilities warrant attention:

- Additional, special, or unanticipated marketing and sales efforts may be required.
- Additional incremental revenue may be generated through sales of the new or refined product.
- Sales of existing products may be affected in either a positive or negative way. If a new product complements an existing product, for example, by expanding its usefulness, the sales impact will be positive. If a new product is a substitute or potential replacement for the existing product, the sales impact will be negative.

Fundamentally, the point is that the development of quarterly sales objectives and estimates of marketing and sales expenses must reflect more than historical relationships and the annual performance goals identified in the planning process; they must also reflect the impact of all research and development activities.

A Gantt chart is a useful way of graphically presenting and managing the timing for the rollout of research and development efforts. The Gantt chart in Exhibit 8-6 has several useful purposes in managing R&D activities. It can show the inherent timing relationships between R&D phases. It can also provide a general indication of when

Exhibit 8-6. Gantt chart for scheduling research and development activities.

OBJECTIVE/PHASE	QUARTER 1			QUARTER 2			QUARTER 3			QUARTER 4			LEVEL OF STAFF SUPPORT	EXPENSES
	MO.	MO.	MO.	MO.	MO.	MO.	MO.	MO.	MO.	MO.	MO.	MO.		
Objective 1														
Conceptualization														
Prototype development														
Prototype testing and refinement														
Pilot market testing														
Final refinement and production														
Full market introduction														
Objective 2														
Conceptualization														
Prototype development														
Prototype testing and refinement														
Pilot market testing														
Final refinement and production														
Full market introduction														
Objective 3														
Conceptualization														
Prototype development														
Prototype testing and refinement														
Pilot market testing														
Final refinement and production														
Full market introduction														
Objective 4														
Conceptualization														
Prototype development														
Prototype testing and refinement														
Pilot market testing														
Final refinement and production														
Full market introduction														

the marketing, sales, and production functions can expect to incur additional work and expense. The sales and marketing impact of the R&D plan can be estimated by assigning a level of staff effort or an expense estimate for each R&D objective and phase. These expenses may be included in either the R&D or the sales section of the forecast, depending on how the company manages the introduction of new products. This format also provides a basis for management control and planning if the timing for milestones is different from that forecast.

Making Final Changes on the Sales and Revenue Plan

The final sales and revenue plan should reflect the operational and financial strategy of the company. Further, it should support the leading-edge efforts of the company and provide the leading indicators of strategic effectiveness. In this regard, the sales and revenue forecast should not be a static effort simply to project sales at one point in the fiscal year.

Sales intelligence can be fully utilized only when it is communicated. Some communication links may be established as a function of the information system. For example, actual monthly sales by product group may be a key input in production and inventory planning. This link may not require extensive personal communication and discussion, but only a tactical effort to produce the required number of units within timing and efficiency constraints. On the other hand, actual monthly and quarterly sales among customer segments may be strategically important to product managers, sales management, and top management. Understanding the reasons for deviation from plans may provide insight into competitor actions, changing customer needs, and necessary strategic or tactical adjustments. This information becomes intelligence when it is discussed and used by management in a strategic manner. The interdisciplinary functions of most companies require management processes that capture and use information as intelligence.

Chapter 9
Developing a Production Plan

The development of a production plan should flow directly from the sales and revenue forecast. The sales objectives represent the first step in defining the outputs that will be required from the company's production unit. In addition to the sales forecast, other information and standards required to develop the production plan include:

- Productivity standards for both labor and equipment
- Production cost standards for specific products and services that reflect the costs of labor and raw materials
- Production capacity and related facilities and equipment costs
- Inventory development and management policies

With the identification of these core standards and policies in place, the specific elements of the production plan can begin to be developed. These include the production schedule, the requirements for and usage of raw materials, the requirements for and utilization of direct production/service labor, the computation and allocation of production/service labor, the computation and allocation of production overhead, and the requirements for capital investment. We will discuss each of these in turn.

Production Scheduling

The first task in developing a production plan is to prepare a production schedule that simultaneously provides for the product output required to support the sales objectives and allows for the realization of efficiencies in the production process. From a production management perspective, a fairly steady and consistent level of production is desirable; this allows for better capacity planning and minimizes the need for frequent, inefficient production changeovers. Of course, this smooth approach may not be ideal if it results in excess inventory.

Production scheduling requires an established set of inventory management policies. These policies necessarily reflect a trade-off among the following factors:

- The costs associated with building and maintaining an inventory that is not immediately translated into sales
- The costs associated with lost sales resulting from unavailability of the product and unwillingness of consumers to wait for it
- The costs associated with fluctuating production levels and frequent production changeovers

A company will probably want to specify minimum and maximum acceptable levels of inventory. The minimum level should be based on the level of confidence and degree of certainty associated with the sales estimates. If there is a significant degree of uncertainty regarding the precise timing of sales, but a high level of confidence regarding the product's ultimate disposition, a company may want to maintain a higher level of inventory to ensure that sufficient quantities of its product are available.

Exhibit 9-1 illustrates how the ABC Corporation developed a production schedule for the product for which it had earlier developed sales objectives. For all but new companies, there will be some beginning level of finished product in inventory. As this exhibit shows, inventory policies can be used to smooth out some of the fluctuations in sales and provide more, but not perfect, consistency in production levels. Of course, ABC may be able to smooth the production process still further if its sales estimates run in a different cyclical pattern, that is, if sales are highest in the first two quarters. If not, the company may have to adopt more flexible inventory management policies.

This approach to production scheduling assumes that a company must plan and execute production in anticipation of sales. Some companies may be able to do this in response to actual sales orders, in which case an existing inventory is not required. In this situation, the company is in a competitive position that allows it to force custom-

Exhibit 9-1. ABC's production schedule.

		Quarter			Total for Year
	1	2	3	4	
1. Sales objective in units	350	525	525	350	1,750
2. Beginning inventory	17.5	49.5	33.5	17.5	—
3. Minimum required ending inventory*	26.5	26.5	17.5	17.5	—
4. Production requirements	359	498	509	350	—
5. Maximum allowed inventory	50	50	50	50	—
6. Ending inventory	49.5	33.5	17.5	17.5	—
7. Production level	382	509	509	350	1,750

*Assume that minimum required inventory equals 5% of the next quarter's sales estimates.

ers to accept a certain amount of lead time while the product is being made. In any event, a production schedule built around the sales forecast is necessary in most cases to plan production capacity properly.

Raw Materials Planning

Raw materials planning involves three determinations. First, the quantities of specific raw materials that will be required to support the levels of production reflected in the production schedule must be determined. Then the company must estimate the average cost per unit of these raw materials and the lead time needed to obtain them.

These determinations depend on the total forecasted production levels by product/service, the usage rates of various raw materials in the production of specific products, and the arrangements with suppliers regarding materials costs, purchase discounts, and delivery scheduling.

For the most part, this information should be developed as part of the internal or external assessments done earlier. Although companies often place heavy emphasis on historical trends, external developments such as competitive developments in supplier markets and the implementation of more efficient production methods must be considered as well.

The first step in the raw materials planning process is to estimate the materials required to support the levels of production demanded by the production schedule. Information about the usage rate of specific raw materials for each unit of finished product is then multiplied by the production requirements to yield an estimate of raw material requirements. This step is illustrated in Exhibit 9-2 for the two raw materials, X and Y, required to make the product for which ABC developed the production schedule shown in Exhibit 9-1. Exhibit 9-2 illustrates the basic relationships involved in computing materials requirements. Companies producing large volumes do not need to compute requirements on a unit-by-unit basis. It is more efficient to develop estimates for a thousand units of finished product than for each unit at a time.

Over the past several years, many manufacturers have been able to both simplify and greatly increase the accuracy of their materials requirements planning (MRP) by

Exhibit 9-2. ABC's estimates of raw materials required (000s omitted).

	Quarter				Total for Year
	1	*2*	*3*	*4*	
1. Production level	382	509	509	350	1,750
2. Material X usage rate	2	2	2	2	—
3. Material X requirements	764	1,018	1,018	700	3,500
4. Material Y usage rate	3	3	3	3	—
5. Material Y requirements	1,146	1,527	1,527	1,050	5,250

making use of an automated MRP system. These software packages, now in their second generation often referred to as MRP II, allow companies to minimize their investment in inventory while still meeting the needs of production by automating the process to a degree or a precision that is usually not possibly manually.

The final step in raw materials planning is to estimate the cost of the raw materials used in the production process. For companies that maintain inventories of raw materials, this step requires planning the inventory of raw materials themselves. The same basic variables are involved in such cases as in planning the inventory of finished products. With information about supplier prices, discounts, and delivery times, a company must make a trade-off decision among the costs of maintaining various inventory levels of specific raw materials, the costs associated with not obtaining bulk-purchased discount prices, and the additional costs incurred in production as a result of running out of key raw materials.

Because the cost of maintaining inventories is so high, new techniques for minimizing this investment are constantly being developed. One well-known and widely followed technique is called just-in-time (JIT). JIT involves working with vendors to arrange delivery of their products at the last possible minute so that purchased inventory goes (almost) directly from the delivery truck onto the production line.

Because costs of raw materials change over time, it is important for a company to know the dollar value of its raw materials inventory and to plan for price methods for valuing inventory. The most common method from a cost management perspective continues to be the first-in, first-out (FIFO) approach. With this approach, the first item to enter inventory is the first item to exit inventory and be used in production. This approach is the easiest method for establishing the value of inventory at the beginning and end of each reporting period. Since, in any given period, production requirements generally exceed beginning inventory, the unit price of ending inventory is the unit price of materials purchased during that period.

Exhibit 9-3 shows how ABC plans inventory and estimates the cost of the requirements developed in Exhibit 9-2 for material X. The exhibit illustrates the impact of inventory value and price increases on raw material costs. As Exhibit 9-3 shows, if a company knows that its supplier(s) will be raising prices, it may want to build up inventories of the affected materials beyond normal levels and thereby reduce overall materials costs. Effective inventory management helps delay the impact of supplier price increases on the cost of finished products.

The output of the raw materials planning process is an estimate of the raw materials costs associated with the level of estimated sales. This output becomes one component of an important concept in both the production plan and the overall business plan—the cost of goods sold.

Direct Labor Planning

Direct labor is the amount of worker time needed to manufacture a product or provide a service. Typically, direct labor should be measured in the smallest practical incre-

Exhibit 9-3. ABC's estimates of raw materials costs (000s omitted).

	Quarter				Total for Year
	1	2	3	4	
1. Material X requirements	764	1,018	1,018	700	3,500
2. Beginning inventory	50	100	370	50	—
3. Unit price of inventory	$ 0.25	$ 0.25	$ 0.25	$ 0.30	—
4. Cost of inventory used	$ 12.50	$ 25.00	$ 92.50	$ 15.00	$145.00
5. Units to be purchased	814	1,288	698	700	3,500
6. Unit price of purchases	$ 0.25	$ 0.25	$ 0.30	—	—
7. Ending inventory*	100	370	50	50	—
8. Cost of purchases used	$178.50	$229.50	$194.50	$195.00	$797.50
9. Value of ending inventory	$ 25.00	$ 92.50	$ 15.00	$ 15.00	—
10. Total cost of materials	$191.00	$254.50	$287.50	$210.00	$942.50

*Minimum ending inventory requirement = 50.

ments of time. Direct labor includes worker supervision but should not include time spent in general management, maintenance, or other support services that cannot be related fairly directly to the production process. Perhaps the best rule of thumb is that any direct labor cost should be one that can be considered a variable expense.

As with planning raw materials, direct labor planning must determine the quantities of specific worker skills that are required to support the levels of production reflected in the production schedule. This determination requires knowledge of two items:

- Labor productivity standards for each of the company's products or services. That is, how much time does it take to manufacture a product or deliver a service? Alternatively, how many product/service units can be delivered for each person-hour of effort?
- Average wage and fringe benefit costs per hour for each worker in each classification or skill category.

This information comes from three sources: historical records; the goals that a company has established regarding productivity; and the company's compensation program, labor agreements, and so on. With this information and the production schedule, an estimate of labor requirements and costs can be developed.

Exhibit 9-4 illustrates ABC's direct labor planning for one worker classification—machinist. A couple of considerations involved in estimating labor requirements and costs, which are reflected here, are that average hourly compensation should include the cost to the company of both wages and fringe benefits and that worker supervision should be included in computing both labor requirements and labor costs. Of course, the exhibit illustrates only one worker classification involved in making the product.

Exhibit 9-4. ABC's estimates of direct labor requirements and costs (000s omitted except for hourly rates).

	Quarter				Total for Year
	1	2	3	4	
1. Production level	382	509	509	350	1,750
2. Machinist—standard hrs./unit	0.2	0.2	0.2	0.2	—
3. Total hours	76.5	102.0	102.0	70.0	350.5
4. Avg. hourly compensation*	$ 6.25	$ 6.25	$ 6.50	$ 6.50	—
5. Total compensation	$478.00	$637.50	$663.00	$455.00	$2,233.50
6. Supervision ratio	1:8	1:8	1:8	1:8	—
7. Supervision hours	9.5	13	13	9	44.5
8. Avg. hourly compensation*	$ 8.50	$ 8.50	$ 8.50	$ 8.50	—
9. Supervision compensation	$ 81.00	$110.50	$110.50	$ 76.50	$ 378.50
10. Total compensation	$559.00	$748.00	$773.50	$531.50	$2,612.00

*Includes fringe benefits at 25% of hourly wage.

Companies must compute these figures for each worker classification involved in the process in order to come up with an estimate of total direct labor requirements and costs.

Production Overhead Planning

The production process costs are not limited to raw materials and direct labor. Additional costs include fixed-cost items, such as space, machine depreciation, general management, and support staff compensation; variable-cost items, such as miscellaneous materials and supplies and maintenance; and combined fixed- and variable-cost items, such as utilities, where cost may consist of both a flat, minimum rate and a usage rate when usage is above a specified level.

The first task in planning production overhead is to identify the fixed-cost items and the fixed-cost components of combined-cost items. By their very nature, these costs are known and constant on a period-to-period basis, allowing for some variability owing to anticipated price increases, salary raises, and the like.

The second task is to identify the variable-cost items and determine from historical records the relationship between these costs and some standard measure of production activity. Standard measures of production activity include production levels, direct labor hours, or machine hours. The appropriate measure may vary with different cost factors. For example, the appropriate measure for miscellaneous materials and supplies may be the production level, while the appropriate measure for maintenance may be machine hours.

It is not necessary when estimating variable overhead costs to associate these costs with production on a unit-by-unit basis; the resulting number is not needed and

Exhibit 9-5. ABC's estimates of production overhead costs (000s omitted).

	Quarter				Total for Year
	1	2	3	4	
1. Production level	382	509	509	350	1,750
2. Direct labor costs	$836.5	$1,115.0	$1,155.5	$794.5	$3,901.5
3. Machine hours	85	91	104	70	350
4. Fixed cost—space	$ 15.0	$ 15.0	$ 15.0	$ 15.0	$ 60.0
5. Gen. mgmt. & staff support	$ 40.0	$ 40.0	$ 40.0	$ 40.0	$ 160.0
6. Utilities	$ 1.0	$ 1.0	$ 1.0	$ 1.0	$ 4.0
7. Total fixed	$ 56.0	$ 56.0	$ 56.0	$ 56.0	$ 224.0
8. Variable cost—miscellaneous materials[1]	$ 2.0	$ 2.5	$ 2.5	$ 1.8	$ 8.8
9. Idle labor time[2]	41.8	55.8	57.8	39.0	194.4
10. Utilities[3]	0.9	0.9	1.0	0.7	3.5
11. Maintenance[4]	8.5	9.1	10.4	7.0	35.0
12. Total variable	$ 53.2	$ 68.3	$ 71.7	$ 48.5	$ 241.7
13. Total overhead	$109.2	$ 124.3	$ 127.7	$104.5	$ 465.7

[1]$5 per 1,000 units of production
[2]5% of direct labor costs
[3]$10 per 1,000 hours of machine time
[4]$10 per 100 hours of machine time

would probably not have much meaning at this point. Because the company has already computed production levels, direct labor hours, and machine hours (although not illustrated, this computation is a logical extension of computing direct labor hours), it merely needs to develop, on the basis of historical relationships, estimates of variable costs associated with these levels of activity.

Exhibit 9-5 illustrates how ABC plans production overhead, using different standard measures of production activity to estimate costs for different variable-cost factors.

The final step in planning production overhead is to allocate total overhead to the units of production. This is an important step in accurately computing total costs per product unit where overhead has been computed for a department that makes more than one product, as is the case in most situations. The easiest approach to allocating overhead is to develop an overhead rate. An overhead rate defines the relationship between the total overhead costs for the production department and some measure of total production activity within that department. For example, if total overhead costs for the year are $750,000 and the department incurs $500,000 in direct labor costs, then the overhead rate is $1.50 per $1.00 of direct labor cost, or 150 percent. In this example, for each $1.00 in direct labor cost associated with a product, the ABC Corporation charges an additional $1.50 in overhead to the cost of each unit of the product.

In recent years, companies have become more aggressive and creative in devel-

Exhibit 9-6. ABC's allocations of overhead expenses (000s omitted except for unit costs).

	Quarter				Total for Year
	1	2	3	4	
1. Production level	382	509	509	350	1,750
2. Direct labor cost—total	$836.50	$1,115.00	$1,155.50	$794.50	$3,901.50
3. Per unit direct labor cost	$ 2.19	$ 2.19	$ 2.27	$ 2.27	—
4. Per unit overhead cost	$ 0.29	$ 0.24	$ 0.25	$ 0.30	—
5. Total overhead cost	$109.20	$ 124.30	$ 127.70	$104.50	$ 465.70

oping complex methodologies for capturing the true total cost of building their product or delivering their service. Such methodologies became more feasible as the result of computerization of the data collection activity as well as of the calculations themselves. The concept of activity-based cost (ABC) developed in response to this trend. Although a detailed discussion of the concepts of ABC is beyond the scope of this book, business planners should be sure that they explore all options, both traditional and nontraditional, for determining costs as part of the planning process.

Exhibit 9-5 illustrates a method for projecting total overhead costs as a first step toward computing an overhead rate. This table assumes a one-product department. Exhibit 9-6 illustrates how the information from Exhibit 9-5 can be used to calculate an overhead rate and compute the overhead expense for each unit of product.

Computing the Cost of Goods Sold

A company should use the various cost estimates that have been developed in the production plan to estimate the total production costs of the products/services that it expects to sell during the year. This estimate is very important in assessing the adequacy of production contribution margins and in preparing the financial plan. The cost of a unit produced is simply the sum total of raw materials cost, direct labor cost, and allocated overhead expense. Computing the cost of goods sold is complicated somewhat by the existence of beginning inventory and the changes in production costs over time. We have discussed the importance of properly valuing inventory. If a company maintains good inventory records, then the cost of goods sold can be computed for each product in the following manner:

Cost of goods sold   = Beginning inventory balance
              + Production expense for period
              − Ending inventory balance

Exhibit 9-7 illustrates how the ABC Corporation computes the cost of goods sold.

Exhibit 9-7. ABC's computation of cost of goods sold (000s omitted).

	Quarter				Total for Year
	1	*2*	*3*	*4*	
1. Beginning inventory—units	17.5	49.5	33.5	17.5	–
2. Beginning inventory	$ 55.0	$ 159.0	$ 106.5	$ 59.0	–
3. Production—units	382.0	509.0	509.0	350.0	1,750.0
4. Production	$1,233.9	$1,618.6	$1,715.3	$1,214.5	$5,782.3
5. Units sold	350.0	525.0	525.0	350.0	1,750.0
6. Ending inventory—units	49.5	33.5	17.5	17.5	–
7. Ending inventory	$ 159.9	$ 106.5	$ 59.0	$ 60.7	–
8. Cost of goods sold	$1,129.0	$1,672.0	$1,762.8	$1,212.8	$5,776.6

	Unit Production Expense by Quarter			
	1	2	3	4
Raw materials	$0.75	$0.75	$0.85	$0.90
Direct labor	2.19	2.19	2.27	2.27
Overhead	0.29	0.24	0.25	0.30
Total	$3.23	$3.18	$3.37	$3.47

Finalizing the Production Plan

Earlier, we discussed the need for congruence between sales objectives and the production capability of the company. In the illustrations in this chapter, we have assumed that sales objectives and production requirements can be achieved given the existing capacity of the company; in other words, no specific expansion of facilities or equipment is required. This will not always be the case; even if existing capacity is sufficient, some replacement or upgrading of equipment may be necessary or desirable.

As part of preparing its production plan, a company should make a list of additional facilities and equipment needs, develop cost estimates for these needs, and factor the estimates into the computation of overhead costs. In some companies, it is desirable to develop alternative overhead budgets that reflect various levels of investment in facilities and equipment. This facilitates an objective financial evaluation of the necessity and desirability of incurring the costs associated with the investments.

Chapter 10
Developing a Financial Plan

The objective of this chapter is to explain the financial planning requirements for a company, differentiate the financial planning requirements for internal-use business plans from those for external use, use information developed in the operating plans to prepare the three major financial statements, and show the impact of operations objectives on the prospective financial position of the company.

The financial plan is the most referred to and, therefore, the most important part of a business plan. The financial plan is often the first part of the business plan the user looks at. If improperly prepared, the financial plan may also be the only part of the business plan the user looks at.

Prospective financial statements are financial statements forecasted or projected into the future on the basis of assumptions regarding future events. Forecasted prospective financial statements reflect management's assumptions as to the conditions it expects to exist and the course of action it expects to take. Projected prospective financial statements are based on management's assumptions about conditions it expects would exist and the course of action it would expect to take given one or more hypothetical assumptions (for example, acquisition of the necessary debt for expanding plant capacity). The assumptions for both forecasted and projected prospective financial statements are based on a combination of available information and judgment in which both the historical performance of the company (if any) and management's plans play a part.

Business plan users will look first at the presentation and accuracy of the prospective financial statements before examining them further. If there are obvious financial presentation or numerical errors, even minor ones, the prospective financial statement user may become concerned about the accuracy of the prospective financial statements and the company's business plan as a whole. If the prospective financial statements are not in an understandable format, this may indicate that the preparer is ignorant of the importance of financial statement preparation.

The prospective financial statements should be prepared in accordance with generally accepted accounting principles (GAAP). A primary reason for creating GAAP was to establish accounting principles that render financial statements comparable as between different entities (especially entities within the same industry) and different accounting periods. For this reason, prospective financial statement users want to see the financial plans presented in accordance with GAAP. The users may want to compare the plan with other financial plans they have analyzed for the same industry or they may want to compare the forecasted or projected results with the financial plans of other potential investments. In either case, generally accepted accounting principles allow for some basis of comparability between financial statements. For this reason, it is best to have a person familiar with GAAP create the prospective financial statements. If such a person is not available from within the company, it may behoove the company to hire a public accounting firm to prepare the prospective financial statements.

In previous chapters we discussed the development of the major components of a company's operating plan—the sales and revenue plan, the production plan, and the organization and management plan. Our approach requires developing plans on the basis of market developments, customer needs, and production capability. However, any company's plans must also be grounded in financial reality, that is, in its ability to finance the operating plan. Sales and production forecasts requiring additional capacity that cannot be financed are useless. Operating plans that result in persistent negative cash positions or continuing losses for the company will not be acceptable to any potential investor. In fact, operating plans that do not allow for a reasonable return to investors or owners probably should not be pursued. The financial plan is key to determining whether an operating plan is feasible. Because of the close interaction between the operating and financial plans, it may require several iterations to achieve consistency between the two. Software spreadsheet packages are available for use with personal computers to shorten the time and simplify the effort required to complete several iterations. We strongly recommend that some form of software spreadsheet be used to make changes efficiently or to run different iterations of the financial plan.

A company's established financial goals and strategy provide the structure for preparing the financial plan. A financial plan generally consists of three financial statements—an income statement, a balance sheet, and a cash flow statement. In addition, the financial plan may include supplemental schedules, such as specific department budgets, the operating results of individual product lines, the financial results of a related entity if this entity is included in the business plan, and financial performance statistics.

Prospective financial statements in a financial plan should be forecasted or projected for from three to five years. Periods longer than five years are often perceived as too speculative, while periods of less than three years are often too short for investors to sense the long-term viability of their investment.

The prospective time units can be monthly, quarterly, or yearly. Monthly financial statements provide a more precise basis for measuring and evaluating the financial feasibility of planned operations. Monthly financial statements are sometimes used by start-up companies with little or no financial history or by companies that have recently emerged from reorganization. Companies with stable operations and a successful financial history may opt to prepare quarterly or yearly financial statements.

Yearly financial statements are usually sufficient for all companies after the second prospective year. As has been emphasized throughout this book, if a company has external uses for the plan, its prospective financial statements should respond to the interests and requirements of the external audiences.

Preparing an Income Statement

An income statement measures the results of a company's operations and financial transactions for a given period of time, whether it be a month, a quarter, or an entire fiscal year. The complete income statement must be developed in two phases. The first phase is to estimate the company's operating income. The second phase focuses on the impact of financing transactions on that operating income. The process must move in two phases because the impact of financing transactions on operating income cannot be computed until the company knows the effect of operations on its balance sheet.

Exhibit 10-1 illustrates the format of an overall income statement, including financial transactions, used by the ABC Corporation. To complete the first phase of the process, ABC has developed estimates of operating income through the planning process. Estimates of revenue, marketing and sales expenses, and cost of goods sold

Exhibit 10-1. ABC's projected income statement (000s omitted).

	Quarter				Total for Year
	1	2	3	4	
Net revenue	$1,680.0	$2,520.0	$2,618.0	$1,748.0	$8,566.0
Cost of sales/goods sold	1,129.0	1,672.0	1,762.8	1,212.8	5,776.6
Gross margin/profit	$ 551.0	$ 848.0	$ 855.2	$ 535.2	$2,789.4
(Marketing and sales expenses	(115.0)	(180.0)	(150.0)	(98.0)	(543.0)
(General and admin. exp.)	(150.0)	(200.0)	(200.0)	(175.0)	(725.0)
(R&D exp.)	(51.5)	(50.0)	(50.0)	(48.5)	(200.0)
Operating income	$ 234.5	$ 418.0	$ 455.2	$ 213.7	$1,321.4
(Interest expense)	–	–	–	–	–
(Depreciation expense)	=	=	=	=	=
Other income (loss)					
Net income (loss) before taxes	=	=	=	=	=
Provision for taxes	–	–	–	–	–
Net income (loss)	=	=	=	=	=

are contained in Exhibits 8-2, 8-3, and 9-7. Estimates of general and administrative expenses appear in Exhibit 7-4. R&D expenses should be estimated on a project-to-project basis. Gross margin is the difference between revenue and the cost of goods sold and should be calculated after the cost of goods sold line on the income statement. It is important that all prospective revenue and expense items be reasonable, based on historical levels. Any large fluctuations between prospective results and historical trends must be explained in the assumptions part of the business plan. Any unexplained or unreasonable variations between prospective financial results and historical trends will lead to skepticism on the part of investors and may make obtaining financing very difficult.

Once operating income has been calculated, interest income, interest expense, and depreciation expense are calculated from the prospective balance sheet. After these items have been calculated, operating income is adjusted to obtain income or loss before taxes. After applying the company's tax rate to income before taxes to obtain the provision for taxes, the net income or loss can be calculated by subtracting the provision for taxes from income before taxes.

Preparing a Balance Sheet

Unlike the income statement, which shows the results of operating and financial transactions for a given time period, the balance sheet shows the financial position of a company at a specific point in time. The basic relationship that must be reflected in a balance sheet is that assets must equal liabilities plus owners' equity. In the simplest terms, assets are items that a company owns or has control of; liabilities are obligations that a company owes; and equity is any excess of assets over liabilities. Exhibit 10-2 illustrates the specific financial items included in each of these categories on the balance sheet. The balance sheet may be the most important financial schedule to an outside investor.

Preparation of a balance sheet is a process that must proceed through several steps: planning working capital, planning capital assets, and planning the financing structure.

Planning Working Capital

All business activity has an impact on the financial accounts included in the balance sheet. The accounts most directly affected are called the working capital accounts, which include current assets and current liabilities. A company's working capital position equals current assets minus current liabilities. Working capital is an important measure of a company's short-term ability to sustain business operations at a viable level. A summary of the impact of an increase in business activity on each of the accounts is presented in Exhibit 10-3.

The specific degree of the impact of operations on the working capital accounts

Exhibit 10-2. A typical balance sheet listing of account names.

Assets	*Liabilities*
Current	Current
Cash	Accounts payable
Short-term investments	Notes payable
Accounts receivable	Wages payable
Notes receivable	Other expenses payable
Inventory	Warranty obligations
Prepaid expenses	Long-term
Long-term investments	Notes payable
Stocks	Other debt/obligations
Funds	
Operational	Owners' Equity
Plant less depreciation	Contributed capital
Equipment less depreciation	Issued stock at par value
Other	Contributed capital in excess of par
Land	Retained earnings
Intangibles	

is determined both by historical relationships and by the company's management policies regarding cash, inventory, and collection and payment periods. For example, a company has historical information about minimum or acceptable levels of inventory, average collection periods, average payment periods, and levels of accrued expenses as a percentage of total expenses or sales. It can use this information to compute expected dollar values in the respective working capital accounts based on the operating plan objectives for sales and revenue, purchases, expenses, and so forth. However, management, if it feels that it is necessary to adjust present policies, may decide to implement tighter inventory management policies to reduce the costs associated with high inventory levels, such as financing costs, storage costs, and potentially higher insurance costs; tighten customer credit policies in order to reduce the average collection period; and negotiate more favorable payment terms with suppliers to extend the average payment period. There will, of course, be trade-offs between the improved cash flow and the long-term effect on customer and vendor relationships involved in each of these policies. Management must give these trade-off decisions careful consideration.

If a company is new and does not have a historical base of information, it can obtain average working capital statistics from such sources as Dun & Bradstreet, Robert Morris Associates, or industry-specific trade associations. A company that is emerging from reorganization may have to improve its historical working capital trends in order to survive. How these improvements will be accomplished must be discussed in the financial plan assumptions.

Developing good estimates of the working capital accounts is a critical step in preparing a valid and reasonable balance sheet and financial plan. In most situations,

Exhibit 10-3. Impact of increased business activity on working capital accounts.

Account	Direction of Change	Reason	Computation
Accounts receivable	Increase	Sales, including credit sales, increase.	$\dfrac{\text{Avg. collection period (in days)}}{\text{Days covered by sales est.}} \times \text{Sales estimate}$
Inventory levels	Generally increase	If standards for minimum levels are used, levels will increase as production increases.	Established as part of the production plan (see Exhibit 9-3 for raw materials inventory and Exhibit 9-7 for finished goods inventory)
Prepaid expenses	Increase	All expenses, including prepaid items (e.g., insurance, taxes), increase.	Depends on nature and timing of prepaid expense items.
Accounts payable	Increase	Purchases, including credit purchases, increase.	$\dfrac{\text{Avg. payment period (in days)}}{\text{Days covered by est. of purchases}} \times \text{Est. of purchases}$
Accrued liabilities	Increase	All expenses, particularly variable ones (e.g., wages), increase.	Must be calculated separately for variable and fixed components. For variable components, historical relationships should be used (e.g., accrued wages as a percentage of total payroll).
Operating cash	Variable, generally increase	Some minimum amount of available cash for emergencies, etc., is desired.	The amount currently on hand and in the company's bank accounts

Exhibit 10-4. ABC's estimates of working capital accounts (000s omitted).

	Quarter			
	1	*2*	*3*	*4*
Income Accounts That Affect Working Capital				
1. Production units	382	509	509	350
2. Net revenue	$1,680.0	$2,520.0	$2,618.0	$1,748.0
3. Purchases	$ 510.0	$ 805.0	$ 525.0	$ 525.0
4. Wages	$ 918.3	$1,210.8	$1,253.3	$ 873.5
5. Other expenses	$ 450.0	$ 585.0	$ 430.0	$ 363.0
Working Capital Accounts				
Assets				
Accounts receivable[1]	$ 560.0	$ 840.0	$ 873.0	$ 583.0
Inventory	210.0	292.0	130.0	100.0
Prepaid expenses	100.0	50.0	75.0	75.0
Total noncash assets	$ 870.0	$1,182.0	$1,078.0	$ 758.0
Liabilities				
Accounts payable[2]	$ 170.0	$ 268.0	$ 175.0	$ 175.0
Accrued wages[3]	147.0	194.0	200.5	140.0
Accrued other expenses[4]	150.0	195.0	145.0	120.0
Total liabilities	$ 467.0	$ 657.0	$ 520.5	$ 435.0
Net noncash working capital	$ 403.0	$ 525.0	$ 557.5	$ 323.0
Operating cash requirements[5]	5.0	8.0	5.0	5.0
Total estimated working capital available	$ 408.0	$ 533.0	$ 567.5	$ 328.0

Note: Above policies are not recommended; they are used for illustration only.
[1]Average collection period = 30 days (accounts receivable = $\frac{1}{3}$ line 2)
[2]Average payment period = 30 days (accounts payable = $\frac{1}{3}$ line 3)
[3]16% of quarterly wages (line 4)
[4]33% of other expenses (line 5)
[5]1% of quarterly purchases (line 3)

changes in working capital accounts define the bulk of the financing requirements for the operating plan. Thus, working capital is the initial link between the operating plan and the financial plan. Exhibit 10-4 illustrates how the ABC Corporation computes estimates in working capital.

Planning Capital Assets

The second step in preparing a balance sheet is to develop estimates of capital assets. Planning capital assets, at least for property, plant, and equipment, is a twofold process. First, the amount of new capital expenditures must be planned. Then, the depreciation of existing fixed assets and any new capital expenditures must be calculated. The combination of these factors yields an estimate of the components of long-term assets. For many companies, this comprises all long-term assets. Some companies, however, may have other long-term assets, including such intangible items as patents, trademarks, copyrights, franchise agreements, licenses, and goodwill.

Plans for new capital expenditures are a direct result of the operating plan. As mentioned earlier, the sales and production plans must consider the company's capacity limitations. Whenever necessary, the production plan must identify additional needs for equipment and facilities. The organization and management plan should include an identification and estimation of costs for the purchase of additional equipment.

Depreciation is a significant aspect of estimating capital assets. Depreciation allocates the cost of a capital asset over its estimated useful life. Depreciation also fulfills the matching principle of accounting, that is, the matching of revenues of a period with all the cost associated with achieving those revenues, including the use of capital assets. The method for depreciating an asset may be straight-line, that is, allocating an equal amount of the capitalized asset value over each period of the asset's useful life. Alternatively, depreciation may be accelerated if management believes that an asset will be more productive during its earlier years of use. Plant and equipment start depreciating the moment they are put into use. Undeveloped land, on the other hand, is usually not depreciated.

As with other capital assets, intangible assets must be amortized over their expected useful life. If the useful life of an intangible asset is undeterminable, the intangible asset must be amortized over a period not exceeding forty years.

Exhibit 10-5 illustrates how ABC has planned its long-term capital assets.

Planning the Financing Structure

The financing structure of the company is composed of the balance sheet items short-term investments, long-term investments, short-term debt, long-term debt, and owners' equity. For planning purposes, it is important to make an end-of-year assessment of the status of these items and then develop estimates of any adjustments to the accounts. This step provides an estimate of interest expenses and interest income that must be used to complete the income statement. It also provides a basis for developing a cash flow summary that will indicate whether planned operations and the current financial structure yield a positive or negative cash flow.

The results of the cash flow analysis determine the required adjustments to the financing structure. These adjustments, in turn, require adjustments to the income statement for interest expense or interest income. Exhibit 10-6 shows ABC's preliminary estimate of the financing structure items of its balance sheet. Once the estimated interest income and interest expense are calculated, the income statement can be finalized, as illustrated in Exhibit 10-7. The cumulative impact of adjustments to the

Exhibit 10-5. ABC's plans for long-term assets (000s omitted).

	Quarter			
	1	2	3	4
Current investment in fixed assets				
Plant	$1,000.00	–	–	–
Equipment	2,000.00	–	–	–
Land	1,500.00	–	–	–
Total	$4,500.00	–	–	–
Planned investment in fixed assets				
Plant	–	$ 25.00	–	–
Equipment	50.00	25.00	–	–
Land	–	–	$ 25.00	–
Total	$ 50.00	$ 50.00	$ 25.00	–
Depreciation on existing assets				
Plant	$ 25.00	$ 25.00	$ 25.00	$ 25.00
Equipment	50.00	50.00	50.00	50.00
Total	$ 75.00	$ 75.00	$ 75.00	$ 75.00
Depreciation on new assets				
Plant	–	–	$ 0.60	$ 0.60
Equipment	–	1.25	1.90	1.90
Total	–	$ 1.25	$ 2.50	$ 2.50
Total depreciation	$ 75.00	$ 76.25	$ 77.50	$ 77.50
Net investment in fixed assets	$4,475.00	$4,448.75	$4,396.25	$4,818.75

financing structure and operational contributions as reflected in the income statement can be translated into quarterly balance sheets, as shown in Exhibit 10-8.

Preparing a Cash Flow Statement

The purpose of a cash flow statement is to evaluate the impact of operations and the financing structure on the cash position of a company. The company must have sufficient cash to cover all its financial obligations at any given point in time. Therefore, it is important for it to know if it will be in a deficit cash position at any point during the year so that it can make arrangements not only to obtain the necessary cash but also to obtain the most favorable financing terms. It is also important for a company

Exhibit 10-6. ABC's preliminary estimates of financing structure items (000s omitted).

	Prior Year Balance	Quarter			
		1	2	3	4
Long-term investment	$ 100	$ 100	$ 100	$ 100	$ 100
Short-term debt	$ 100	$ 75	$ 25	–	–
Long-term debt	$1,500	$1,500	$1,480	$1,480	$1,460
Owner's contributed capital	$3,250	$3,250	$3,250	$3,250	$3,250
Retained earnings	$ 250	$ 250	$ 250	$ 250	$ 250
Interest earned[1]		–	$ 10	–	$ 10
Interest paid[2]		$ 55	$ 55	$ 55	$ 55
Debt retired		$ 25	$ 70	$ 25	$ 20

[1]For the purpose of this exhibit, retained earnings are assumed to be constant. However, when the estimated financial statements are finalized, the quarterly retained earnings will change to reflect quarterly net income.
[2]These figures, based on the financing structure, are needed to complete the income statement that appears in Exhibit 10-7.

Exhibit 10-7. ABC's completed income statement (000s omitted).

	On a Numerical Basis Quarter				Total for Year
	1	2	3	4	
Revenue	$1,680.0	$2,520.0	$2,618	$1,748	$8,566.0
(Cost of sales/goods sold)	(1,129.0)	(1,672.0)	(1,752.8)	(1,212.8)	(5,766.6)
Gross margin/profit	551.0	848.0	855.2	535.2	2,789.4
(Marketing and sales expenses)	(115.0)	(180.0)	(150.0)	(98.0)	(543.0)
(General and admin. exp.)	(150.0)	(200.0)	(200.0)	(175.0)	(725.0)
(R&D expenses)	(51.5)	(50.0)	(50.0)	(48.5)	(200.0)
Operating income	234.5	418.0	455.2	213.7	1,321.4
(Interest expense)	(55.0)	(55.0)	(55.0)	(55.0)	(220.0)
(Depreciation expense)	(75.0)	(76.2)	(77.5)	(77.5)	(306.2)
Other income (loss)	–	10.0	–	10.0	20.0

(continued)

Exhibit 10-7. (*continued*)

	On a Numerical Basis Quarter				Total for Year
	1	*2*	*3*	*4*	
Net income (loss) before taxes	104.5	296.7	322.7	91.2	815.1
Provision for taxes @ 40%	41.8	118.7	129.1	36.5	326.1
Net income (loss)	$ 62.7	$ 178.0	$ 193.6	$ 54.7	$ 489.0

	On a Percent of Revenue Basis Quarter				Total for Year
	1	*2*	*3*	*4*	
Revenue	100.0%	100.0%	100.0%	100.0%	100.0%
Cost of sales/goods sold	67.2	66.3	67.3	69.4	67.4
Gross margin/profit	32.8%	33.7%	32.7%	30.6%	32.6%
(Marketing and sales expenses)	(6.9)	(7.1)	(5.7)	(5.5)	(6.3)
(General and admin. expenses)	(8.9)	(7.9)	(7.6)	(10.0)	(8.5)
(R&D expenses)	(3.0)	(2.0)	(1.9)	(2.9)	(2.3)
Operating income	14.0%	16.6%	17.4%	12.2%	15.4%
(Interest expense)	(3.3)	(2.2)	(2.1)	(3.1)	(2.6)
(Depreciation expense)	(4.5)	(3.0)	(3.0)	(4.4)	(3.6)
Other income (loss)	–	0.4	–	0.6	0.2
Net income (loss) before taxes	6.2%	11.8%	12.3%	5.3%	9.5%
Provision for taxes	2.5	4.7	4.9	2.1	3.8
Net income (loss)	3.7%	7.1%	7.4%	3.2%	5.7%

to know how much excess cash it will have so that it can use that cash to pay down existing liabilities, invest in capital assets, or invest in other income-producing assets.

The cash flow statement is broken down into three sections: cash flows provided by (used in) operating activities; cash flows provided by (used in) investing activities; and cash flow provided by (used in) financing activities. These three sections are then followed by a summary section of net cash flow containing the increase or decrease

Exhibit 10-8. ABC's unclassified balance sheet: Summary of end-of-quarter status (000s omitted).

Account Name	Prior Year Balance	Quarter			
		1	2	3	4
Assets					
Cash	$ 95	$ 159	$ 171	$ 361	$ 707
Accounts receivable	540	560	840	873	583
Inventory	70	210	292	130	100
Prepaid expenses	165	100	50	75	75
Long-term investments	100	100	100	100	100
Long-term assets, net	4,500	4,475	4,448	4,396	4,319
Total assets	$5,470	$5,604	$5,901	$5,935	$5,884
Liabilities and Owners' Equity					
Liabilities					
Accounts payable	$ 150	$ 170	$ 268	$ 175	$ 175
Short-term debt	100	75	25	—	—
Accrued wages	120	147	194	201	140
Accrued other	100	150	194	145	120
Long-term debt	1,500	1,500	1,480	1,480	1,460
Total liabilities	1,970	2,042	2,161	2,001	1,895
Owners' equity					
Contributed capital	3,250	3,250	3,250	3,250	3,250
Retained earnings	250	312	490	684	739
Total owners' equity	3,500	3,562	3,740	3,934	3,989
Total liabilities and owners' equity	$5,470	$5,604	$5,901	$5,935	$5,884

in cash for the period, the cash and cash equivalents at the beginning of the year, and the cash and cash equivalents at the end of the year.

Cash flows provided by (used in) operating activities begins with net income or loss. To net income or loss are added depreciation and amortization expenses, which are noncash charges. Accounts receivable, inventory, and prepaid expenses follow in that order; any increases in these accounts from the prior period are considered a cash outflow, and any decrease a cash inflow. Accounts payable and accrued expenses follow, with increases in these accounts considered cash inflows and decreases considered cash outflows.

The cash flows provided by (used in) investing activities section usually consists of any purchases or sales of capital assets. Purchases of capital assets for cash are

Exhibit 10-9. ABC's quarterly cash flow statement (000s omitted).

	Quarter			
	1	2	3	4
Cash flows provided by operating activities				
Net earnings	$ 62	$179	$194	$ 55
Adjustments to reconcile net earnings to net cash provided by (used in) operating activities:				
Depreciation	75	76	77	77
Changes in assets and liabilities:				
Accounts Receivable decrease; (increase)	(20)	(280)	(33)	290
Inventory decrease; (increase)	(140)	(82)	162	30
Prepaid Expenses decrease; (increase)	65	50	(25)	0
Accounts Payable increase; (decrease)	20	98	(93)	0
Accrued Expenses increase; (decrease)	77	91	(42)	(86)
Net cash provided by operating activities	139	132	240	366
Cash flow used in investing activities:				
Purchase of long-term assets	(50)	(50)	(25)	0
Net cash used in investing activities	(50)	(50)	(25)	0
Cash flows provided by (used in) financing activities:				
Proceeds from long-term debt	0	0	0	0
Payments on long-term debt	(25)	(70)	(25)	(20)
Net cash used in financing activities	(25)	(70)	(25)	(20)
Net increase in cash and cash equivalents	64	12	190	346
Cash and cash equivalents at the beginning of the year	95	159	171	361
Cash and cash equivalents at the end of the year	$159	$171	$361	$707

considered a cash outflow, while cash proceeds from the disposal of a capital asset are considered a cash inflow. Any gain or loss from the sale of a capital asset recorded in the income statement is considered a cash inflow or a cash outflow, respectively, in this portion of the cash flow statement.

The cash flows provided by (used in) financing activities section includes any borrowing (cash inflow) or any paydown of borrowed principle (cash outflow). This section also includes any payment of dividends (cash outflow), any cash received from the sale of stock (cash inflow), or any payment for the purchase of treasury stock (cash outflow).

Net cash flow is the net cash flow provided by (used in) operating, investing, and financing activities. Exhibit 10-9 shows a very favorable short-term cash position for the ABC Corporation. The company's operations are generating a significant amount

Exhibit 10-10. Summary of ABC's planned year-end financial performance (000s omitted).

Liquidity	=	Current assets / Current liabilities	=	$1,633.9 / $435.0	= 3.76
Inventory utilization	=	Cost of goods sold / Avg. inventory	=	$5,766.6 / 335.0	= 17.20
Fixed asset utilization	=	Sales / Avg. net fixed assets	=	$8,566.0 / $4,409.4	= 1.94
Total asset utilization	=	Sales / Avg. total assets	=	$8,566.0 / $5,886.3	= 1.46
Debt	=	Total Debt / Avg. total assets	=	$1,895.0 / $5,886.3	= 0.32
Profit margin on sales	=	Net Profit / Sales	=	$407.6 / $8,566.0	= 0.04
Return on total assets	=	Net Profit / Avg. total assets	=	$407.6 / $5,886.3	= 0.06
Return on common equity	=	Net Profit / Avg. owners' equity	=	$407.6 / $3,953.8	= 0.10
Average collection period	=	Receivables / Annual sales ÷ 360	=	25 days	

of cash owing to a strong gross margin from the existing product mix and to limited additional investments in operational assets.

Finalizing a Financial Plan

The preceding process produces final income statements, balance sheets, and cash flow statements.

A company may take an additional step to finalize its financial plan by preparing a statistical summary of its planned financial performance to determine if the performance is consistent with the goals and objectives established in the planning process. Some indicators that can be used to evaluate the financial performance of the company are shown in Exhibit 10-10.

To summarize, the financial plan is intimately linked to the operating plans. The process for developing a financial plan, which has been described in this chapter, illustrates how the objectives from the operating plans are used to build the financial objectives. ABC's operating objectives were financially viable for the company. In other situations, the operating objectives may generate cash deficits that cannot be covered by the company using either internal or external sources of cash. When a company cannot finance a deficit, it must reevaluate and refine its operating plans until they become financially viable. This interactive process between operating and financial objectives will probably have to go through several iterations.

Chapter 11
Pulling the Plan Elements Into a Finished Product

The purpose of this chapter is to identify and describe the elements of a well-organized business plan, to discuss how to customize the plan for its intended user, and to explain how best to present a business plan to third parties.

The preparation of a formal plan document has several objectives. First, the document brings closure to the planning process. Although planning should be an ongoing activity for any company, the document reflects the decisions that have been made to guide the company over a specified period of time. Second, the document formalizes the objectives and strategies that have been developed through the planning process as operating policies of the company. It provides an easy mechanism for communicating these policies to people both inside and outside the company. Finally, the document is a tangible management tool that can be used to evaluate subsequent activities, accomplishments, and opportunities as well as the assumptions on which the planning decisions were based.

Plan Format and Content

The substance of the plan document should flow fairly directly from the operating and financial plans already made. Exhibit 11–1 is a suggested outline for a plan document. The rest of this chapter describes in detail how the plan should be organized and what each section should contain.

Exhibit 11-1. Outline of a business plan document.

I. Title page
  A. Name of company
  B. Time period covered by plan
  C. Date of preparation

II. Table of contents

III. Executive summary
  A. The company and its environment
  B. Current position and outlook
  C. Goals
    1. Financial
    2. Nonfinancial
  D. Strategies
    1. Marketing and sales
    2. Production
    3. Research and development
    4. Organization and management
    5. Finance

IV. Sales and revenue plan
  A. Sales and revenue objectives
  B. Product/service line strategies
    1. Target customers
    2. Sales objectives
    3. Pricing policies
    4. Advertising, promotion
    5. Distribution
  C. Marketing and sales organization

V. Production plan
  A. Production schedule
  B. Production costs and standards
    1. Materials
    2. Labor
  C. Operating policies
    1. Inventory management
    2. Maintenance
    3. Purchasing
    4. Subcontracting
  D. Facilities
  E. Capital expenditures

VI. Research and development plan
  A. Assignment of responsibilities
  B. Management plan
    1. Objectives
    2. Expenses

VII. Organization and management plan
  A. Organizational structure
  B. Management policies and objectives
    1. General philosophy
    2. Recruitment and selection
    3. Training and development
    4. Compensation
  C. Position descriptions (if appropriate and needed)
  D. Résumés

VIII. Financial plan
  A. Schedules
    1. Income statements
    2. Balance sheets
    3. Cash flow summary
    4. Financial performance summary
    5. Departmental budgets
      a. Marketing and sales
      b. Production
      c. Research and development
      d. Administration
  B. Policies
    1. Debt management
    2. Investments
    3. Use of earnings
    4. Profit sharing

Title Page and Table of Contents

The document should have a title page that states the name of the company, the time period covered or addressed by the plan, and the date of final preparation of the document. If the plan is to be used to raise funds, the time frame may be best defined in terms of periods—for instance, year 1, year 2, first quarter, second quarter—rather than in terms of specific dates (so that the plan will not become quickly outdated). The table of contents, following the title page, identifies each major section of the plan and the page number on which that section begins. If appropriate, a list of exhibits should also be included in the table of contents.

Executive Summary

In general, the executive summary presents an overview of the company and the highlights of the completed business plan. Specifically, the executive summary should include the following five subsections:

1. *The history of the company:* A brief description of the company's formation, how it has developed, what its historical strengths and weaknesses have been, and who its major player(s) are.
2. *The company and its environment:* A brief description of the company, its purpose in the marketplace (what it is trying to do for whom in terms of providing products or services), its general product/service lines, and the factors that affect its operation and success.
3. *Current position and outlook:* An assessment of the company's current market position and its potential for growth and improvement. The description should address the company's strengths and weaknesses and the perceived outlook in terms of threats and opportunities. It should also look at competitors' strengths and weaknesses and how the competition has reacted to changes in the market.
4. *Goals:* A list and brief explanation of the improvement goals and objectives that the company has established for the period covered by the plan.
5. *Strategies:* Brief descriptions of the major thrusts and improvement actions to be taken in each of the components of the plan—for example, marketing and sales, production, and finance. This should be done with reflection on the company's recent history and its goals for the future.

The purpose of the executive summary is to present highlights and a brief but informative overview of what the company is and where it is going. In general, the executive summary should not exceed four to five pages in length.

Sales Plan

The sales and revenue plan should identify planned sales in terms of both units and unit prices to achieve the forecasted revenue. To be a useful management tool, the sales and revenue plan should also describe the assumptions that underlie the marketing and sales objectives and decisions.

The sales and revenue plan should include the following items:

- A schedule of annual sales and revenue objectives differentiated by product/ service lines. (If appropriate, this information can be broken down into monthly or quarterly periods.)
- A description of marketing strategy for each product/service line in terms of the market size, major customers, pricing strategy and discount policies, advertising and promotion efforts, distribution networks, and so forth
- A budget for marketing and sales expenses differentiated by product/service lines
- An outline of marketing and sales responsibilities describing how the marketing and sales effort will grow as the company's revenue base expands and how the marketing and sales effort will diversify to meet the challenges of new products/services offered by the company and/or its competitors
- Descriptions of the key personnel involved in the marketing effort

Production Plan

The production plan identifies planned production levels and outlines the basic production or operations strategy for achieving these levels. As with the sales and revenue plan, the production plan should describe the assumptions that underline the production objectives and decisions. The main assumptions are the costs of direct materials and direct labor, indirect manufacturing costs, fixed and variable overhead costs, the allocation of overhead costs, and productivity standards.

The description of the production plan should include the following information:

- An overview of the major machinery and technologies involved in the manufacturing process.
- A schedule of annual production objectives differentiated by product/service lines. (If appropriate, this information can be broken down into monthly or quarterly periods.)
- Productivity and production cost standards for each product/service line.
- Inventory management policies for direct materials and finished goods.
- Equipment utilization and maintenance policies.
- A description of the production facilities, including identification of any additions that may be needed to expand production capability, diversify products/

services, or replace outdated machinery. Capital expenditures that may be required to maintain production capability must also be considered.

Research and Development Plan

When appropriate and applicable, the R&D plan identifies specific objectives, the budget for the period covered by the plan, and the assignment of responsibilities for R&D activities. Description of the R&D plan should include:

- An outline of where R&D efforts are being focused, that is, whether the thrust is new product development, improved product quality, increased production output, or reduced production costs
- Information on the backgrounds and skills of key players in the R&D function, description of the R&D facilities, and identification of the person who is ultimately responsible
- Specification of the decision-making authority for what R&D pursues, when a new product is ready to be marketed, and when cost-saving technology is ready to be introduced to the production facility

Organization and Management Plan

The organization and management plan identifies the organizational structure of the company and describes its policies, standards, and objectives for developing and managing its human resources.

The organization and management plan should include the following items:

- A statement of the company's general management philosophy
- An organizational chart
- A description of the authority and responsibilities of the various positions within the company
- Productivity measures and standards for the various positions within the company
- Policies and procedures for recruitment and selection of personnel, training and development, and compensation
- The company's labor relations policies
- Specification of significant employee or union contracts, together with a summary of contract contents and a schedule of when contracts are due to expire
- Identification of new positions that may be required as the company grows and/or diversifies

If the business plan has external uses, brief résumés of key personnel should also be included.

Financial Plan

The financial plan summarizes the expected financial performance and position of the company as affected by the operations plans. The financial plan should include the following prospective financial information:

- Monthly, quarterly, or yearly income statements
- Monthly, quarterly, or yearly balance sheets
- Monthly, quarterly, or yearly cash flow summaries
- Monthly, quarterly, or yearly summaries of financial performance
- Supplemental schedules with monthly, quarterly, and yearly departmental budgets prepared for marketing and sales expenses, production expenses, and administrative expenses

These financial schedules provide the framework for evaluating the financial viability of a company's operations on a go-forward basis in both the planning and the implementation phases. Additionally, the company's historical financial statements and transactions may be included. These will be required in any financing situation but may not be necessary for internal purposes.

Along with the schedules, the financial plan should state the assumptions used in preparing the financial schedules, such as the accounts receivable collection cycle, the trade payable payment cycle, the inventory turnover ratio, depreciation methods, the expected interest rates on debt financing, and major income tax issues.

Finally, the financial plan should also describe the company's policies for using financial leverage, evaluating investment opportunities, paying dividends, and using excess cash.

Appendices

Most business plans should also include selected appendices to fill out the information base on key elements of the plan. The specific nature and types of appendices vary, depending on the company and the intended uses of the plan. For example, plans that are prepared in anticipation of raising funds should put detailed budgets in an appendix rather than in the body of the financial plan. Other examples of material that might appropriately be included in an appendix are the results of the external assessment and the related market data that support marketing and sales objectives; the résumés of key personnel; and demographic information.

Customizing the Plan for Its Intended User

Every business plan, we repeat, should be tailored to its user. If the business plan is being prepared for lenders, investors, or internal users, the outline presented in Exhibit 11-1 is an excellent guide. The users of the plan will want as much information as possible on which to base their decisions. However, all segments of the outline may not be necessary. For example, service companies may not have a research and development function. And small companies may have such a flexible organizational structure that it will suffice merely to mention it and include the résumés of key employees. Business planners will have to use their own discretion in deciding what will meet the needs of the prospective users of the plan. If the planner is unsure, a rule of thumb is that too much detail is always better than not enough detail. But regardless of the plan user, the financial plan portion of the business plan will always be necessary and should always be prepared in a proper accounting format.

Presenting the Plan to Third Parties

As with most introductions, it is important that the plan make a good first impression when it is unveiled before users. The plan should look professional, preferably bound in a folder bearing the company logo. If such folders do not exist, the plan can be bound in a window folder with the name of the company and the contents on it. If the financial planner does not have access to a binding machine, a local copying company should be able to do the binding. Avoid the appearance of a book and use color and graphics whenever possible to enhance the readability and appearance of the document.

All plans sent to users through the mail should be accompanied by a transmittal letter explaining what the package is and including a phone number and a name to call if the reader has any questions. The cover letter should also tell users that they will be contacted within a week to arrange a time to meet and discuss the contents of the plan.

Ultimately, an oral presentation of the business plan may be called for, for example, in the case where the business plan has been prepared for purposes of raising capital. If this is expected, the plan itself should be structured so that the same schedules, graphics, and financial information contained in the plan can be used again as overheads, slides, or handouts in the oral presentation. Likewise, the flow of the presentation should be the same as in the document. In any case, as with any presentation, the presenter must believe in the material for it to be effective.

APPENDIX
SAMPLE BUSINESS PLAN

XYZ CO., Inc. BUSINESS PLAN December 31, 19X9

Prepared November 30, 19X8

TABLE OF CONTENTS

EXECUTIVE SUMMARY

XYZ Co., Inc. (the Company) is one of the leading widget manufacturers in the United States. Widgets are a key component in the complex circuitry required for high technology products. The Company provides many of the largest high-tech manufacturers with high-quality, reasonably priced widgets. The management team is seeking an investor and additional management expertise to take the Company to the next level of revenue and profitability.

XYZ Company History

XYZ Co. was founded in 19W4 in Jersey City, New Jersey, specializing in the manufacturing of low-volume, high-end widgets. The Company did reasonably well but slowly fell behind competitors that could design as well as manufacture widgets.

XYZ Co. hired Mr. David Kenney as operating manager in 19W8 and promoted him to the position as chief operating officer in 19W9. Mr. Kenney had spent several years designing widgets for a competitor before joining XYZ Co. Although Mr. Kenney's design capabilities enabled the Company to expand its customer base, he became frustrated with stagnation facing the Company in New Jersey and purchased it in 19X2. He immediately moved it to Winchester, Massachusetts, hoping to forge close ties with New England educational institutions that were on the cutting edge of advanced circuitry.

Mr. Kenney succeeded in forging ties with two institutions, Plope Institute of Technology (PIT) and Mystic University. These contacts enabled the Company to increase sales in 19X3 and 19X4 and led to exponential sales growth from 19X5 through 19X7.

Mr. Kenney passed away suddenly in 19X8. The Company is now owned by Mrs. Freda Land, acting president, and Mr. John Land, chief financial officer.

The Company and Its Environment

XYZ Co. makes both specially manufactured and mass-produced widgets for the high-technology market, primarily consumer electronics and computers. XYZ Co. can either design and manufacture widgets for customers or can simply manufacture widgets from designs provided by customers. The Company has never designed widgets to be manufactured elsewhere.

Specialized manufacturing techniques are necessary to produce widgets used in the high-end mainframe computer market, which requires great speed, power, and accuracy. These widgets are usually designed by the customer with final design modifications and testing of prototypes performed by XYZ Co.'s engineers in conjunction with the customers' engineers.

After discussions with customers, lower-end widgets are usually designed and tested by XYZ Co. through the final prototype phase. Final prototypes are then approved by customers before the Company begins production runs.

The major factor that determines the success of the Company is its ability to produce widgets efficiently with a moderately paid, semi-skilled workforce. XYZ Co. is currently a low-cost producer that relies heavily on employee manufacturing flexibility. Flexibility on the part of the Company's employees is necessary due to the complex nature of widget manufacturing and the fact that widgets have a low dollar value in the marketplace, which makes highly specialized labor inefficient. This flexibility has been nurtured by large, ongoing investments in employee training.

The Company is a nonunion shop and there has never been an effort to unionize at XYZ Co. Based on the experience of the Company's competitors, if XYZ Co. ever unionized it might lose some of its manufacturing flexibility and efficiency.

Current Position and Outlook

Currently, XYZ Co. is the most highly regarded widget manufacturer in the United States in terms of quality of manufacturing and of design. Although there are larger manufacturers in terms of sales volume (the Company currently has a 5% share of the total domestic widget market), none are as strong in design nor can any produce widgets as efficiently as XYZ Co.

Although U.S. widget manufacturers are facing increasing competition from overseas suppliers, XYZ Co. does not feel threatened by foreign competition because of its superior design capabilities, efficient manufacturing techniques, and cheap distribution costs. XYZ Co. is also quicker to respond to customer needs than foreign competition is because of its proximity to customer purchasers.

Management feels that a potential threat to widget manufacturers is the increasing tendency of high-tech manufacturers to design and manufacture widgets in-house, vertically integrating an aspect of manufacturing that was previously reserved for specialty manufacturers like XYZ Co. However, management also feels that the downward pressure on widget prices and its ability to manufacture efficiently insulates the Company from losing present customers, which probably could not design and manufacture high-quality widgets as cheaply as they can buy them from XYZ Co.

The best opportunity for XYZ Co. lies in overseas markets. Because of its international reputation for excellence—established at domestic trade shows attended by overseas high-tech manufacturers—management feels that the Company could easily expand sales and production into Europe and/or Asia. Entering overseas markets would require clearing certain hurdles. Although management feels that obtaining ISO 9000 Certification would be relatively easy, expertise in foreign sales strategies, foreign currency hedging, and overseas distribution channels would be needed before entering overseas markets. These markets also would require additional capacity in plant, equipment, and human resources. Management feels that an investment in overseas expansion would provide a large return and feels such an investment is worth pursuing.

Objectives

Management feels that the Company is sound financially and that it is the most efficient manufacturer of widgets in the United States. Management wishes to seize the opportunity to expand overseas, a market that would increase gross sales by approximately 35 percent within five years of entry. Equally important, the Company must adjust after the loss of Mr. Kenney.

Therefore, management's objectives are twofold. One, the Company needs a President with international expertise to guide it through ISO 9000 requirements, devise overseas sales and manufacturing strategies, help structure overseas distribution channels, and develop an overall strategy for the Company. Two, the Company needs an equity investor(s) who can provide the capital necessary to implement overseas sales, manufacturing, and distribution strategies.

Strategy

Management plans to maintain the Company's superior market position by keeping investments in fixed assets, research and development, and marketing higher than industry norms. Management intends to maintain current sound fiscal policies and current profitability while acquiring the resources necessary to enter overseas markets.

XYZ COMPANY HISTORY

XYZ Co. was the vision of Mr. David Kenney, who designed widgets for one of the first widget manufacturers on the East Coast after obtaining an engineering degree from Hope University. Widgets are a key component in the complex circuitry required for high technology products. After several years of designing widgets, Mr. Kenney left to obtain a master's degree in business administration from Brice University. Upon graduating from Brice in 19W8, Mr. Kenney went to work for XYZ Co., originally as operations manager and later becoming the chief operating officer as well.

Mr. Kenney bought XYZ Co. in 19X2, took the additional title as president, and moved operations to Winchester, Massachusetts, the following year, hoping to capitalize on the high technology research being done in New England by institutions such as Plope Institute of Technology and Mystic University. Mr. Kenney and XYZ Co. forged close ties with these institutions and as the high-tech industry started growing, so did XYZ Co., establishing a reputation for designing and manufacturing high-quality widgets at reasonable prices.

As computers and other high-technology equipment became cheaper through the use of mass production and automated manufacturing techniques, XYZ Co. expanded; it produced not only specially designed, low-volume widgets but also simpler widgets that could be mass-produced cheaply while maintaining their high quality.

XYZ Co. grew slowly through 19X4 then grew exponentially from 19X5 through 19X7 because of rising high-technology sales in the United States.

Mr. Kenney passed away suddenly in 19X8. XYZ Co. came under the present management of Mrs. Freda Land, Mr. Kenney's sister, and Mr. John Land, Mrs. Land's husband. Freda Land owns 75 percent of XYZ Co.'s stock while John Land owns 25 percent. Mrs. Land and Mr. Land have been active in XYZ Co. since Mr. Kenney moved to the Company to Winchester, Massachusetts.

SALES AND MARKETING

XYZ Co. is considered the highest-quality widget manufacturer in the United States. XYZ Co. can either manufacture widgets according to customer designs or it can both design and manufacture widgets. All widgets are made to order and picked up by customers upon completion.

Management follows the strategy of using its own sales force of engineers, who fully understand the engineering behind widget design and manufacturing, instead of hiring manufacturing sales representatives. In recent years, the Company has spent most of its sales resources on deeply penetrating its existing customer base as opposed to getting new customers. Pricing for the Company's widgets are usually slightly lower than the competition because of XYZ Co.'s manufacturing efficiencies.

XYZ Co. has a tremendous customer base. Because of the Company's ability to both manufacture and design widgets, it can accommodate both high-volume, high-tech manufacturers who have their own design teams and smaller high-tech manufacturers who cannot afford their own design teams. The Company's customers are in the computer, consumer electronics, medical, and scientific industries. Some of the major customers include:

JCN Computers, Inc.	Life Support, Inc.
TIMM Systems, Inc.	Test Labs, Inc.
Electrovaxe, Inc.	Environmental Testers, Inc.
Electronix, Inc.	Medical Labs, Inc.

The diversity of the Company's customer base prevents XYZ Co. from relying on any one customer for a disproportionate share of sales.

Because of the manufacturing requirements of its customers, XYZ Co.'s sales tend to be seasonal. Historically, demand for the Company's widgets is stronger during its second and third fiscal year quarters. This is due to consumer high-tech customers who manufacture heavily during the months of August through October in order to stock up for Christmas sales. These customers like to have their widgets inventoried before their busy manufacturing season begins. Table A provides the historical per-

Table A. Percentage of total sales by quarter.

	Quarter				Total Units Sold During Year (000s Omitted)
	1	2	3	4	
19X5	20	30	35	15	1,000
19X6	20	25	35	20	1,250
19X7	20	25	35	20	1,400
19X8					
Forecast	20	30	30	20	1,750

Table B. Unit and dollar sales by quarter (000s omitted).

	Unit and Dollar Sales by Quarter				Total for Year
	1	2	3	4	
Units	350	525	525	350	1,750
Avg. unit prices	$ 5.00	$ 5.00	$ 5.25	$ 5.25	—
Sales	$1,750.00	$2,625.00	$2,755.00*	$1,840.00*	$8,970.00

*Rounded to nearest $5.

centage of unit sales by quarter as well as the estimated percentage of unit sales by quarter for the forecast period.

Table B provides an estimate of unit sales by quarter for the forecast period. The estimate of unit sales is net of returns which, because of outstanding manufacturing quality, are minimal. Sales figures are in gross dollars and do not include discounts. All forecasts in this business plan reflect estimates for XYZ Co.'s core business, domestic widgets. It does not include any estimates of overseas widget sales. Management feels that within five years of entering overseas markets, XYZ Co. would increase its gross sales by 35 percent.

Table C provides an estimate of net sales for the four quarters ending December 31, 19X9, after taking into consideration average sales discounts provided to customers. Sales discounts are given to the Company's largest customers for the production efficiency accompanying large orders. These discounts are then averaged across quarterly sales to obtain the average discount rate per quarter used when calculating net revenue.

Most of the Company's revenue comes from its existing customer base. Although new customers are cultivated through trade shows, trade publications, and word of

Table C. Discounted sales by quarter (000s omitted).

	Sales by Quarter				Total for Year
	1	2	3	4	
Sales	$1,750	$2,625	$2,755	$1,840	$8,970
Discount %	4	4	5	5	—
Total discount	$ 70	$ 105	$ 137	$ 92	$ 404
Net sales	$1,680	$2,520	$2,618	$1,748	$8,566

Table D. Historical sales and variable sales expenses (000s omitted).

Factor	19X6	19X7	19X8	19X9 (Forecast)
Sales	$4,900	$6,387	$7,627	$8,970
Variable sales expenses	$ 100	$ 130	$ 150	$ 180
Variable promotion expenses	50	70	85	100
Variable distribution expenses	20	25	30	53
Total variable marketing expenses	$ 170	$ 225	$ 260	$ 333
Variable marketing expense to sales ratio	3.47%	3.52%	3.41%	3.71%

mouth from existing customers, XYZ Co. does not expend significant resources to attract new customers. Because of its prestigious client base and its manufacturing capacity limitations, XYZ Co. currently operates at over 90% capacity in both capital and human manufacturing resources, most of the sales and marketing efforts are spent maintaining close relationships with existing customers.

XYZ Co. currently employs six salespeople, including a chief sales engineer, Ms. Laura Lopez. All six salespeople have engineering degrees, which allows them to interact easily with customers' engineers and purchasers. Each salesperson has his or her own territory strategically located around existing customers' purchasing offices. Ms. Lopez is responsible for coordinating the technical capabilities in design, production, and bid analysis. All salespeople report to Ms. Lopez on a weekly basis. There is a monthly sales meeting attended by all salespeople and Mrs. Land, the acting president, at the Company's headquarters in Winchester, Massachusetts.

Table E. Marketing and sales expense by quarter (000s omitted).

	Marketing and Sale Expenses by Quarter				Total for Year
	1	2	3	4	
Quarterly sales	$1,750	$2,625	$2,755	$1,840	$8,970
Variable marketing expense to sales ratio	3.71%	3.73%	3.70%	3.70%	3.71%
Variable marketing expenses	$ 65	$ 98	$ 102	$ 68	$ 333
Fixed expenses	30	30	30	30	120
Special events expenses	20	52	18	—	90
Total marketing and sales expenses	$ 115	$ 180	$ 150	$ 98	$ 543

Table D shows the historical relationship between sales and variable expenses for XYZ Co.

Table E gives XYZ Co.'s quarterly estimates of marketing and sales expenses for the forecast period.

XYZ Co.'s geographic markets include all the high-technology hot spots in the United States. The breakdown of salespeople by region follows:

Region	Sales People
California	2
Texas	1
Midwest	2
North Atlantic	1

PRODUCTION AND TECHNICAL CAPABILITIES

XYZ Co. produces widgets that are used by original equipment manufacturers in the computer, consumer electronic, medical, and scientific industries. A related use is for commercial and industrial testing equipment. Order sizes vary from small production runs of specifically designed widgets to large production runs of less complex widgets.

XYZ Co. has its only manufacturing facility in Winchester, Massachusetts. This plant is run by Mr. Patrick Homes, chief operating officer. Mr. Homes began with the Company in 19W3 and worked his way through the ranks, replacing Mr. Kenney as chief operating officer by 19X4. Mr. Homes is considered a leading expert in widget manufacturing in the United States and is an important reason for XYZ Co.'s manufacturing efficiency.

Mr. Homes maintains a high ratio of production supervisors to production workers, one supervisor to every eight production workers, in order to quickly resolve any problems on the shop floor. Mr. Homes runs the plant with a bare minimum of inventory. This is possible because of the fine relationship he developed with the suppliers during his tenure as Purchasing Supervisor, enabling XYZ Co. to implement a just-in-time inventory management system. Mr. Homes also started the policy of training XYZ Co. suppliers in aspects of quality control to improve the Company's own manufacturing efficiency. Under Mr. Homes' tenure as chief operating officer, XYZ Co. has cut its average cycle time for designing and producing widgets over 50 percent: from forty days to just under twenty days.

Operations

Production engineering, planning, and scheduling involves the engineering analysis, modification, and timing of each job order. In a job shop system, this typically includes a unique set of production requirements and processes for each order, which may involve any or all of the company's technical and production capabilities. The Company is currently implementing a bar code scanning system to schedule and track work in process and improve shop floor control. Table F provides the production schedule for XYZ Co. for the forecast period concerning estimated sales and desired ending inventory levels.

The purchasing function is responsible for raw materials inventory management

Table F. XYZ's production schedule (000s omitted).

	Quarter				Total for Year
	1	2	3	4	
1. Sales objective in units	350	525	525	350	1,750
2. Beginning inventory	17.5	49.5	33.5	17.5	—
3. Minimum required ending inventory*	26.5	26.5	17.5	17.5	—
4. Production requirements	359	502	509	350	—
5. Maximum allowed inventory	50	50	50	50	—
6. Ending inventory	49.5	33.5	17.5	17.5	—
7. Production level	382	509	509	350	1,750

*Assume that minimum required inventory equals 5% of the next quarter's sales estimates.

and usage analysis. The purchasing supervisor is also responsible for receiving raw materials and finished goods, and related dock control. The Company plans to automate its purchasing function to further improve the management of this area. A just-in-time inventory management system was recently implemented to reduce inventory holding costs while minimizing raw materials shortages. Because XYZ Co. manufactures to order, finished goods inventory is not maintained. In most cases, customers' goods are picked up on the final day of a production run. Table G gives the estimated raw material requirements for the forecast period considering raw materials necessary for each unit manufactured.

Quality control, inspection, and testing includes preproduction analysis, production inspection, and quality control over finished goods. Review and modification of designs are discussed with clients prior to production scheduling. During production, testing is performed at critical production stages. Final electronic tests are coordinated with an outside testing source to independently verify the compliance of production to original design specifications. XYZ Co. has invested in testing equipment and training to assure a high degree of compliance in its production process. Table H gives the estimate of production overhead costs for XYZ Co. during the forecast period. The table indicates the basis of overhead cost and calculates total fixed overhead, total variable overhead, and total overhead costs.

Table I provides the estimate of total overhead cost by quarter for each unit produced during the forecast period.

Production Supervision involves the shop floor management of job production. XYZ Co. supervisors are directly involved in production to assure a high level of quality, provide cross-training of production staff, and maintain safety in the work place. Table J provides the estimate of direct labor costs for XYZ Co. during the forecast period. Average compensation includes fringe benefits of 25 percent of hourly wages. Supervision ratios are based on historical norms and current levels. Production supervisors also oversee machine and shop maintenance to maintain a high level of efficiency.

Table K gives the total cost of goods sold and the per unit cost of goods sold for each quarter of the forecast period.

Table G. XYZ's estimates of raw materials requirements (000s omitted).

	Quarter				Total for Year
	1	2	3	4	
1. Production level	382	509	509	350	1,750
2. Material X usage rate	2	2	2	2	—
3. Material X requirements	764	1,018	1,018	700	3,500
4. Material Y usage rate	3	3	3	3	—
5. Material Y requirements	1,146	1,527	1,527	1,050	5,250

Table H. XYZ's estimates of production overhead cost (000s omitted).

		1	2	3	4	Total or Year
		Quarter				*Total or Year*
1.	Production level	382	509	509	350	1,750
2.	Direct labor costs	$836.5	$1,115.0	$1,155.5	$794.5	$3,901.5
3.	Machine hours	85	91	104	70	350
4.	Fixed cost—space	$ 15.0	$ 15.0	$ 15.0	$ 15.0	$ 60.0
5.	Gen. mgmt. & staff support	$ 40.0	$ 40.0	$ 40.0	$ 40.0	$ 160.0
6.	Utilities	$ 1.0	$ 1.0	$ 1.0	$ 1.0	$ 4.0
7.	Total fixed	$ 56.0	$ 56.0	$ 56.0	$ 56.0	$ 224.0
8.	Variable cost—miscellaneous materials[1]	$ 2.0	$ 2.5	$ 2.5	$ 1.8	$ 8.8
9.	Idle labor time[2]	$ 41.8	$ 55.8	$ 57.8	$ 39.0	$ 194.4
10.	Utilities[3]	$ 0.9	$ 0.9	$ 1.0	$ 0.7	$ 3.5
11.	Maintenance[4]	$ 8.5	$ 9.1	$ 10.4	$ 7.0	$ 35.0
12.	Total variable	$ 53.2	$ 68.3	$ 71.7	$ 48.5	$ 241.7
13.	Total overhead	$109.2	$ 124.3	$ 127.7	$104.5	$ 465.7

[1]$5 per 1,000 units of production
[2]5% of direct labor costs
[3]$10 per 1,000 hours of machine time
[4]$10 per 100 hours of machine time

Table I. XYZ's allocations of overhead expenses (000s omitted except for unit costs).

	1	2	3	4	Total for Year
	Quarter				*Total for Year*
1. Production level	382	509	509	350	1,750
2. Direct labor cost—total	$836.50	$1,115.00	$1,155.50	$794.50	$3,901.50
3. Per unit direct labor cost	$ 2.19	$ 2.19	$ 2.27	$ 2.27	—
4. Per unit overhead cost	$ 0.29	$ 0.24	$ 0.25	$ 0.30	—
5. Total overhead cost	$109.20	$ 124.30	$ 127.70	$104.50	$ 465.70

Table J. XYZ's estimates of direct labor requirements and costs (000s omitted except for hourly rates).

	Quarter				Total for Year
	1	2	3	4	
1. Production level	382	509	509	350	1,750
2. Machinist—standard hrs./unit	0.2	0.2	0.2	0.2	—
3. Total hours	76.5	102	102	70	350.5
4. Avg. hourly compensation*	$ 6.25	$ 6.25	$ 6.50	$ 6.50	—
5. Total compensation	$478.00	$637.50	$663.00	$455.00	$2,233.50
6. Supervision ratio	1:8	1:8	1:8	1:8	—
7. Supervision hours	9.5	13	13	9	44.50
8. Avg. hourly compensation*	$ 8.50	$ 8.50	$ 8.50	$ 8.50	—
9. Supervision compensation	$ 81.00	$110.50	$110.50	$ 76.50	$ 378.50
10. Total compensation	$559.00	$748.00	$773.50	$531.50	$2,612.00

*Includes fringe benefits at 25% of hourly wage.

Table K. XYZ's computation of cost of goods sold (000s omitted).

	Quarter (000s Omitted)				Total for Year
	1	2	3	4	
1. Beginning inventory—units	17.5	49.5	33.5	17.5	—
2. Beginning inventory	$ 55.0	$ 159.0	$ 106.5	$ 59.0	—
3. Production—units	382.0	509.0	509.0	350.0	1,750
4. Production	$1,233.9	$1,618.6	$1,715.3	$1,214.5	$5,782.3
5. Units sold	350.0	525.0	525.0	350.0	1,750
6. Ending inventory—units	49.5	33.5	17.5	17.5	—
7. Ending inventory	$ 159.9	$ 106.5	$ 59.0	$ 60.7	—
8. Cost of goods sold	$1,129.0	$1,671.1	$1,762.8	$1,212.8	$5,775.7

	Unit Production Expense by Quarter			
	1	2	3	4
Raw materials	$0.75	$0.75	$0.85	$0.90
Direct labor	2.19	2.19	2.27	2.27
Overhead	0.29	0.24	0.25	0.30
Total	$3.23	$3.18	$3.37	$3.47

Technical Capabilities

XYZ Co.'s technical capabilities have developed as its customer base and sales volume have grown. When Mr. Kenney purchased the company in 19X2, it produced only complex widgets on small production runs. Since then, capabilities have expanded to include the designing and manufacturing of simple, high-quality widgets that can be mass-produced. The technical disciplines performed by XYZ include:

- Etching
- Plating
- Lamination
- Fabrication
- Photo production
- Computerized step and repeat

- Automatic and hand screening
- Chemical laboratory and failure analysis
- CNC drilling and coordinated digitizing
- Inspection
- Pollution control
- Safety

The key pieces of equipment that increase the efficiency of the production process include:

- Automatic mask screener
- CNC drilling with magnetic media loading
- Kouvar welder to repair multilayer panels
- CAD computer system for use in step and repeat production and digitizing
- Drill disk-a-tapes to increase drilling efficiency
- State of the art waste treatment deionization system
- Back-up equipment in multilayer, printing, screening, laminating, plating, and drilling
- Plating tanks

Increases in productivity could result from expanding plating tanks and integrating step and repeat capabilities in the production of design circuitry. However, plant, equipment, and human resources are presently operating at over 90 percent utilization and further production gains by the above efficiencies would be minimal.

Plant and Equipment Requirements

Because of regular maintenance of existing plant and equipment overseen by the production supervisors, frequent updating of existing equipment, and continuous purchases of needed equipment, there are no significant purchases of plant and equipment required at XYZ Co. manufacturing facility. However, because of the 90% utilization of plant and equipment mentioned earlier, if XYZ Co. desired to expand its current production levels, additional capital expenditures would be required.

RESEARCH AND DEVELOPMENT

Management of XYZ Co. believes in substantial investments in research and development (R&D) in order to stay on the leading edge of widget design and manufacturing. Industry trade publications indicate that XYZ Co. has invested more in R&D per net revenue dollar than any of its competitors have for the past three years. That trend is expected to continue during the forecast period and management has forecasted R&D expenditures to be over 2 percent of net revenue. See Table L for the forecasted quarterly R&D budget.

Mr. Michael Dells heads the research and development department of XYZ Co. In addition to Mr. Dells, XYZ Co. has five engineers on staff. Each engineer designs widgets for customers and is required to spend numerous hours in the XYZ Co. research and development laboratory experimenting in advanced widget design and building prototypes using these advanced designs. Engineers also experiment with different materials attempting to increase manufacturing efficiencies and/or widget durability. Mr. Dells' research and development projects are often the result of discussions Company salespeople have with clients regarding products using new types of circuitry or new materials in the products' advanced circuitry.

New product breakthroughs are discussed with the chief operating officer and production supervisors. If production can be accomplished efficiently, salespeople are given training regarding the pros and cons of the new product. Salespeople then approach customers in their territory for feedback regarding the new product. If customer reaction is favorable, joint meetings are held with management, engineers, production supervisors, and salespeople to determine product viability and pricing. Once viability and pricing are established, the new product is offered to customers.

Another thrust of research and development over the years has been employee training. Mr. Kenney believed that a well-trained work force experienced in numerous manufacturing tasks enables employees to fill in wherever needed on the shop floor. This gives XYZ Co. manufacturing flexibility superior to that of competitors. Training sessions for employees are usually conducted in-house by the Company's engineers and/or material and equipment vendors. Employee training is the primary reason

Table L. Estimated research and development expenditures for the forecast period.

Resources	Quarter				Total for Year
	1	2	3	4	
Staff hours	3,400	1,100	3,400	1,000	8,900
Staff cost	$21,250	$ 6,875	$21,250	$ 6,500	$ 55,875
R&D expense	$30,250	$43,125	$28,750	$42,000	$144,125
Total expense	$51,500	$50,000	$50,000	$48,500	$200,000

that employee turnover at XYZ Co. is low and productivity rates are high compared to industry norms.

Table L provides a detailed breakdown of research and development expenses for the forecast period.

ORGANIZATION AND MANAGEMENT

At XYZ Co., management feels that its open-door management philosophy allows for a free exchange of ideas among all levels and divisions of the Company. It is this exchange of ideas that has made XYZ Co. the most efficient widget manufacturer in the U.S.

XYZ Co. has been managed with a minimum of administrative and overhead costs. Presently, 89 people are employed by the Company. The breakdown of employees within each of the major employment groups is as follows:

Employment Group	*Employees*
Executive management	2
Accounting, personnel, and records	3
Sales	6
Production engineering, planning, and scheduling	8
Purchasing, shipping, and receiving	2
Quality control, inspection, and testing	2
Production supervision	8
Production staff	58
Total full-time employees	89

Executive management includes the acting president and chief financial officer.

Work Force

The management of XYZ Co. is proud of the team that comprises its work force. Management feels that its most important employees are its salespeople, production supervisors, production staff, and engineers.

All salespeople have engineering degrees. This allows them to easily interact with customers' engineers and purchasers. Laura Lopez, the senior salesperson, was made chief sales engineer shortly after Mr. Kenney's death to coordinate technical capabilities in design, production, and bid analysis, all tasks previously performed by Mr. Kenney. Compensation for the sales force consists of a base salary and commissions based on sales with extra bonuses for exceeding sales quotas.

Production supervisors, all groomed from within the organization, are paid an annual salary with bonuses tied to the meeting of production goals. All were personally trained by Mr. Kenney and have a strong sense of loyalty to XYZ Co.

Production staff includes semiskilled production workers from the northern metropolitan area. Production staff are competitively paid, conscientious in their work activities, and productive. Additional production staffing can be drawn from a large metropolitan area pool of semiskilled and unskilled labor. Training for production staff is available through internal training programs.

The Company's engineers are trained in widget design and manufacturing techniques by Mr. Homes, chief operating officer, and Mr. Dells, head of research and development. Although the primary responsibility of all engineers is designing widgets for customers, a significant portion of each engineer's time is devoted to research and development. All engineers are APICS certified. Each engineer is paid an annual salary plus bonuses based on any original research and development concept that develops into a new product.

The work force of XYZ is not represented by organized labor and turnover is not a problem. The pension obligation is fully funded and there is currently no profit-sharing plan.

Key Personnel

The key personnel involved with XYZ Co. include Mrs. Freda Land, acting president; Mr. John Land, chief financial officer; Mr. Patrick Hŏlmes, chief operating officer; Mr. Michael Dells, head of research and development; and Ms. Laura Lopez, chief sales engineer. These five form the management team of XYZ Co. and meet bimonthly to discuss company events and strategy.

Mrs. Freda Land

Mrs. Land has been the controller of XYZ Co. since 19X2. She graduated from Brice University in 19X4 with an undergraduate degree in accounting. She spent eight years at Cronin, Donnelly, Ferland, and Kennedy (CDF&K), a large regional accounting firm located in northern New Jersey, where she obtained her certified public accounting (CPA) license and reached the level of senior manager.

Since joining XYZ Co., Mrs. Land has been responsible for all financial accounting functions and clerical administration. Upon the death of Mr. Kenney, she also took the title of acting president.

Mr. John Land

Mr. Land has been the chief financial officer (CFO) of XYZ Co. since 19X2. He graduated from Blake University in 19V5 and received an MBA from Maynard University in 19V9. He went to work with Cronin, Donnelly, Ferland, and Kennedy until 19W6. While at CDF&K Mr. Land earned his CPA license and obtained the title of manager.

In 19W7, Mr. Land left CDF&K and went to work as CFO of Stills Brewery in

Hoboken, New Jersey. As CFO he turned the financially troubled organization into one of the most profitable regional breweries on the East Coast.

In addition to his position as CFO, Mr. Land is also the human resource manager.

Mr. Patrick Homes

Mr. Homes is the chief operating officer of XYZ Co. Mr. Homes joined the Company in 19W3 starting on the shop floor. He left the Company in 19W5 to obtain an engineering degree from the Cas School of Engineering and Applied Sciences at the University of New Haven in New Haven, CT.

Upon completion of his studies, Mr. Homes returned to XYZ Co. and became a production supervisor and later purchasing supervisor. He was promoted to design engineer in 19X3 and to chief operating officer in 19X4. Mr. Homes is considered a leading expert in widget manufacturing and is currently on the Massachusetts Board of High Technology Manufacturers, an organization devoted to attracting high technology manufacturers to Massachusetts.

Mr. Michael Dells

Mr. Dells is the head of research and development at XYZ Co. Mr. Dells obtained an undergraduate engineering degree from Brice University, a master's in engineering with a concentration in material sciences from Wyatt Institute of Technology, and a doctorate in applied sciences from Mystic University.

Mr. Dells joined XYZ Co. in 19X1 as an engineer and had worked for a competitor of XYZ Co. for several years before that. He was named head of research and develop-

Table M. XYZ's functional organization chart.

```
                    ┌─────────────────┐
                    │  Mrs. Freda Land │
                    │ Acting President/│
                    │    Controller    │
                    └─────────────────┘
                             │
     ┌───────────────┬───────┴───────┬───────────────┐
┌────────────┐ ┌──────────────┐ ┌──────────────┐ ┌──────────────┐
│Ms. Laura   │ │Mr. Michael   │ │Mr. Patrick   │ │Mr. John Land │
│Lopez       │ │Dells         │ │Homes         │ │Chief Financial│
│Chief Sales │ │Head of       │ │Chief         │ │Officer       │
│Engineer    │ │Research      │ │Operating     │ │              │
│            │ │and Development│ │Officer       │ │              │
└────────────┘ └──────────────┘ └──────────────┘ └──────────────┘
```

ment in 19X5. Although Mr. Dells has no full-time staff, all XYZ Co. engineers are required to spend a portion of their time working for Mr. Dells in the Company's research and development laboratory.

Ms. Laura Lopez

Ms. Lopez is XYZ Co.'s chief sales engineer. She obtained her engineering degree from Plope Institute of Technology (PIT) in 19X2. Since joining XYZ Co. Ms. Lopez has earned an MBA with a concentration in marketing from PIT.

Ms. Lopez was the first salesperson hired by Mr. Kenney. She joined XYZ Co. in 19X2 and has been instrumental in the Company's growth. Upon the death of Mr. Kenney, Ms. Lopez was named chief sales engineer. Although her primary responsibilities include coordinating technical capabilities in design, production, and bid analysis, Ms. Lopez has kept a small sales territory for herself in order to stay in touch with customer needs and the widget market.

Table M is the current functional organization chart for XYZ Co.

FINANCIAL PLAN

XYZ Company, Inc.
FINANCIAL STATEMENT INFORMATION
Forecasted Year Ending December 31, 19X9

The following financial statement information presents the forecasted balance sheets, income statement, and cash flow statement of XYZ Company, Inc. for the year ended December 31, 19X9. All financial statement information was prepared by the management of XYZ Co. Historical financial statements for years 19X7 and 19X8 are presented in Exhibit A.

The forecasted financial information presents, to the best of management's knowledge and belief, the expected results of operations for the four quarters ending December 31, 19X9 assuming that:

1. XYZ's marketing and sales efforts generate the projected revenues.
2. The capital structure and expense relationships remain as anticipated.

The forecast reflects management's judgment of the expected conditions and its expected courses of action if the above assumptions are accurate and achieved. The presentation is intended to provide information for potential investors and cannot be considered a presentation of expected future results, since the terms of financing, and new management objectives will inevitably alter the assumptions used for the presentation. Please refer to the accompanying notes to this presentation to assess the appropriateness of specific assumptions. Because this presentation displays ongoing assumptions, it may not be useful for other purposes. Even if the assumptions are accurate, there will usually be differences between estimated and actual results because events and circumstances frequently do not occur as expected, and these differences may be material.

NOTE A—BACKGROUND AND SUMMARY OF ACCOUNTING POLICIES

XYZ's Co.'s presentation of estimated financial information is based on its historical costs of operation and sales trends. The company is entirely operational and ongoing with regard to manufacturing capability and capacity. This presentation is based on current circumstances and conditions and does not assume any changes in capital structure that might result from additional investment.

NOTE B—SUMMARY OF SIGNIFICANT ASSUMPTIONS

1. *Source*

All estimates and assumptions have been made by the current stockholders of XYZ Co.: Mrs. Freda Land and Mr. John Land.

2. *Assets*

Cash includes all short-term investments with maturities of 3 months or less.

The accounts receivable balance at the balance sheet date is assumed to be 33 percent of quarterly net sales based on historical quarterly relationships and estimates of future collectibility. This represents a collection cycle of approximately 30 days.

Inventories include work-in-process and raw materials, based on historic inventory levels. No finished goods inventories are included since XYZ Co. operates a custom job shop and completed goods are picked up by customers for current payment as produced.

Property, plant, and equipment (PP&E) include furniture and fixtures, production equipment, office equipment, tooling, vehicles, and leasehold improvements. The PP& E balance at each balance sheet date incorporates the additions assumed by management to be necessary to support the sales volume. XYZ Co. depreciates all equipment on a straight-line basis over their expected useful life.

Prepaid expenses are estimated based on XYZ Co.'s current relationship with its insurers.

3. *Liabilities*

The accounts payable consists of trade payables. Accounts payable are estimated to fluctuate between 10 and 15 percent of cost of goods sold based on historic quarterly relationships.

Accrued wages are assumed by management to be approximately 26 percent of direct labor based on historical relationships.

Accrued other is estimated based on its historical quarterly relationships with operating expenses, ranging from 35 to 45 percent.

Income taxes are assumed to be paid as incurred. For that reason there are no accrued income taxes on the balance sheet.

Short-term debt consists of a shareholder loan made in 19X6. The loan is scheduled to be fully repaid in the second quarter of 19X9. Interest is calculated at 12 percent per year.

Long-term debt consists of a balloon loan from ABC Bank. Interest is calculated based on a rate of prime plus 2 percent per year. The loan is scheduled to mature in 19Y5 but can be extended by the bank if XYZ Co. is in compliance with its loan covenants. XYZ Co. is currently in compliance with all loan covenants.

4. *Shareholder's Equity*

Common stock includes 10,000 shares outstanding at a par value of $325 per share.

5. *Revenue*

Revenue is recorded when orders are shipped. Net sales are assumed to increase at a rate of approximately 17 percent annually, based on the results of the year ended December 31, 19X8 and current market information concerning the growth in the widget manufacturing industry.

6. *Cost of Goods Sold*

The components of cost of goods sold include direct materials, direct labor, depleted chemicals, and manufacturing overhead. Direct material, direct labor, and depleted chemicals cost are assumed to vary directly with the volume of sales. A reduction in manufacturing overhead as a percentage of sales is assumed during the period of presentation, since some of the expenses included in cost of goods sold are step-variable or fixed within the range of sales and operations presented.

7. *Operating Expenses*

Operating expenses include marketing and sales, general and administrative, and research and development expenses. For the year ending December 31, 19X9, these components as a percentage of net sales are estimated as follows:

Marketing and sales expense	6.3%
General and administrative expense	8.5
Research and development expense	2.3
Operating expenses as a percentage of sales	17.1%

8. *Income Tax Expense*

Management assumes a combined federal and state income tax rate of 40 percent of net income before taxes for each of the periods shown in the presentation.

XYZ COMPANY, INC.
FORECASTED BALANCE SHEET

QUARTERS ENDING
DECEMBER 31, 19X9
(000s Omitted)

	QUARTER 1	*QUARTER 2*	*QUARTER 3*	*QUARTER 4*
ASSETS				
Cash	$ 160	$ 171	$ 361	$ 707
Accounts receivable	560	840	873	583
Inventory	210	292	130	100
Prepaid expense	100	50	75	75
Land	100	100	100	100
Property, plant, and equipment net of depreciation	4,474	4,448	4,396	4,319
Total assets	$5,604	$5,901	$5,935	$5,884
LIABILITIES AND OWNERS' EQUITY				
Liabilities				
Accounts payable	$ 170	$ 268	$ 175	$ 175
Short-term debt	75	25	0	0
Accrued wages	147	194	201	140
Accrued other	150	194	145	120
Long-term debt	1,500	1,480	1,480	1,460
Total liabilities	2,042	2,161	2,001	1,895
Owners' equity				
Contributed capital	3,250	3,250	3,250	3,250
Retained earnings	312	490	684	739
Total owners' equity	3,562	3,740	3,934	3,989
Total liabilities and owners' equity	$5,604	$5,901	$5,935	$5,884

XYZ COMPANY, INC.
FORECASTED INCOME STATEMENT

QUARTERS ENDING
DECEMBER 31, 19X9
(000s Omitted)

	QUARTER 1	QUARTER 2	QUARTER 3	QUARTER 4	TOTAL FOR YEAR
Sales	$1,680	$2,520	$2,618	$1,748	$8,566
Cost of goods sold	(1,129)	(1,672)	(1,763)	(1,213)	(5,777)
Gross profit	551	848	855	535	2,789
Marketing and sales expense	(115)	(180)	(150)	(98)	(543)
General and administration expense	(150)	(200)	(200)	(175)	(725)
Research and development expense	(52)	(50)	(50)	(49)	(201)
Operating profit	234	418	455	213	1,320
Interest expense	(55)	(55)	(55)	(55)	(220)
Depreciation expense	(75)	(76)	(78)	(77)	(306)
Other income	0	10	0	10	20
Net income before taxes	104	297	322	91	814
Provision for taxes @ 40%	(41)	(119)	(128)	(36)	(324)
Net income	$ 63	$ 178	$ 194	$ 55	$ 490

XYZ COMPANY, INC.
FORECASTED STATEMENT OF CASH FLOWS

	QUARTERS ENDING DECEMBER 31, 19X9 (000s Omitted)				TOTAL FOR YEAR
	QUARTER 1	QUARTER 2	QUARTER 3	QUARTER 4	
Cash flows provided by operating activities:					
Net income	$ 63	$178	$194	$ 55	$490
Adjustments to reconcile net earnings to net cash provided by operating activities:					
Depreciation	75	76	78	77	306
Change in assets and liabilities:					
Accounts receivable	(20)	(280)	(33)	290	(43)
Inventory	(140)	(82)	162	30	(30)
Prepaid expenses	65	50	(25)	0	90
Accounts payable	20	98	(93)	0	25
Accrued expenses	77	91	(43)	(86)	39
Net cash provided by operating activities	140	131	240	366	877
Cash flows used in investing activities:					
Property, plant, and equipment	(50)	(50)	(25)	0	(125)
Net cash used in investing activities	(50)	(50)	(25)	0	(125)
Cash flows provided by (used in) financing activities:					
Payments on long-term debt	0	(20)	0	(20)	(40)
Payments on short-term debt	(25)	(50)	(25)	0	(100)
Received from (Distributions to) stockholders	0	0	0	0	0
Net cash used in financing activities	(25)	(70)	(25)	(20)	(140)
Net increase in cash and cash equivalents	65	11	190	346	612
Cash and cash equivalents at the beginning of the period	95	160	171	361	95
Cash and cash equivalents at the end of the period	$160	$171	$361	$707	$707

EXHIBIT A
KEY FINANCIAL RATIOS

XYZ Co. Forecasted Key Ratios for the Period Ending December 31, 19X9

Liquidity	=	$\dfrac{\text{Current assets}}{\text{Current liabilities}}$	=	$\dfrac{\$1,465}{\$435}$	=	3.37
Inventory utilization	=	$\dfrac{\text{Cost of goods sold}}{\text{Avg. inventory}}$	=	$\dfrac{\$5,777}{\$85}$	=	68
Fixed asset utilization	=	$\dfrac{\text{Sales}}{\text{Avg. net fixed assets}}$	=	$\dfrac{\$8,566.0}{\$4,409.5}$	=	1.94
Total asset utilization	=	$\dfrac{\text{Sales}}{\text{Avg. total assets}}$	=	$\dfrac{\$8,566}{\$5,677}$	=	1.51
Debt	=	$\dfrac{\text{Total Debt}}{\text{Avg. total assets}}$	=	$\dfrac{\$1,460}{\$5,677}$	=	0.26
Profit margin on sales	=	$\dfrac{\text{Net Profit}}{\text{Sales}}$	=	$\dfrac{\$489}{\$8,566}$	=	0.06
Return on total assets	=	$\dfrac{\text{Net Profit}}{\text{Avg. total assets}}$	=	$\dfrac{\$489}{\$5,677}$	=	0.09
Return on common equity	=	$\dfrac{\text{Net Profit}}{\text{Avg. owners' equity}}$	=	$\dfrac{\$489.0}{\$3,744.5}$	=	0.13
Average collection period	=	$\dfrac{\text{Receivables}}{\text{Annual Sales} \div 360}$	=	25 days		

EXHIBIT B
HISTORICAL FINANCIAL STATEMENTS

XYZ COMPANY, INC.
BALANCE SHEET

	YEARS ENDING DECEMBER 31, (000s Omitted)	
	19X8	19X7
ASSETS		
Cash	$ 95	$ 19
Accounts receivable	539	478
Inventory	70	53
Prepaid expense	166	125
Land	100	100
Property, plant, and equipment net of depreciation	4,500	4,575
Total assets	$5,470	$5,350
LIABILITIES AND OWNERS' EQUITY		
Liabilities		
Accounts payable	$ 150	$ 144
Short-term debt	100	138
Accrued wages	120	120
Accrued expenses	100	85
Long-term debt	1,500	1,746
Total liabilities	1,970	2,233
Owners' equity		
Contributed capital	3,250	3,250
Retained earnings	250	(133)
Total owners' equity	3,500	3,117
Total liabilities and owners' equity	$5,470	$5,350

XYZ COMPANY, INC.
INCOME STATEMENT

	YEARS ENDING DECEMBER 31, (000s Omitted)	
	19X8	19X7
Sales	$7,284	$6,100
Cost of goods sold	(5,099)	(4,111)
Gross profit	2,185	1,989
Marketing and sales expense	(459)	(427)
General and administrative expense	(619)	(549)
Research and development expense	(168)	(153)
Operating profit	939	860
Interest expense	(240)	(262)
Depreciation expense	(75)	(100)
Other income	15	9
Net income before taxes	639	507
Provision for taxes @ 40%	(256)	(203)
Net income	$ 383	$ 304

XYZ COMPANY, INC.
STATEMENT OF CASH FLOWS

	YEARS ENDING DECEMBER 31, (000s Omitted)	
	19X8	19X7
Cash flows provided by operating activities		
Net income	$383	$304
Adjustments to reconcile net earnings to net cash provided by operating activities:		
Depreciation	75	100
Change in assets and liabilities		
Accounts receivable	(61)	(100)
Inventory	(17)	(15)
Prepaid expense	(41)	(30)
Accounts payable	6	8
Accrued expense	15	5
Net cash provided by operating activities	360	272
Cash flows used in investing activities		
Long-term assets	0	0
Net cash used in investing activities	0	0
Cash flows provided by (used in) financing activities		
Payments on long-term debt	(246)	(250)
Payments on short-term debt	(38)	(30)
Net cash used in financing activities	(284)	(280)
Net increase in cash and cash equivalents	76	(8)
Cash and cash equivalents at the beginning of the year	19	27
Cash and cash equivalents at the end of the year	$ 95	$ 19

Index